DANCING

WITH

DIFFERENCES

Janet Desautels

MOtivational PRESS®
LEADERS IN GLOBAL PUBLISHING

Published by Motivational Press, Inc.
1777 Aurora Road
Melbourne, Florida, 32935
www.MotivationalPress.com

Manufactured in the United States of America.

ISBN: 978-1-62865-239-0

CONTENTS

Expressions of Gratitude 6

CHAPTER ONE   Vive la Difference! 9

  Separate and Apart? 13

  Dancing with Differences 15

  Let's Meet in the Field 17

  Goodwill toward Men 20

  The Beauty of Adversity 24

CHAPTER TWO   Many Worlds 26

  The Other 32

CHAPTER THREE   Cultural Differences: One Difference to Rule Them All . . 33

  Universals? 42

  You Say Tomay-to, I Say Tomah-to...Let's Call the Whole Thing Off 43

  Barriers: Through the Looking Glass 47

CHAPTER FOUR   Allowing 50

  When Others Don't Make Sense 51

  As Within, So Without: A Shift in Perspective 57

  What Is, Is 61

CHAPTER FIVE   How to Accept and Allow: 64

  Stories

  The Power of Story 64

  Destiny 69

  The Possibility in Critical Thinking 69

  The Power of Belief 71

  Judging Others' Beliefs 72

  To Assume or Not to Assume—That is the Question 77

Culture Is a Story about 'Us' 80

Whose Story Are You Taking On? Taking Things Personally. 81

Listen To Understand

How To Accept and Allow: 85

Acknowledging Humanity 87

Listening: The Great Defuser 92

Listening for the Unspoken. 94

Be Here Now

How to Accept and Allow: 102

The Dissolution of Stories and Judgements from the Past 102

The Peace of Not Thinking 112

Appreciation

How To Accept and Allow: 113

How Do I Appreciate the 'Tough' Cases? 115

CHAPTER SIX   Using Thought and Energy on Purpose **118**

Personal Power and Responsibility 123

Unseeing the Big Dipper. 126

The Good News: It's Not Hard Work 128

Choice 129

The Feeling of Thoughts 132

Switching on the Fly: Replacing Negative with Positive. 133

Problem-Solving 137

What We Focus on Grows 138

A Different Story about Desire 139

A Recipe for Success 141

The Power of Intention 143

What You Put in You Get Out 145

CHAPTER SEVEN   One Person at a Time **147**

The Little Will Be Great 147

Just One Heart 148

This book is about how to handle all your differences and conflicts with others, whether they are based in culture, opinion, or personality. While it's nice to seek common ground with others to get along, sometimes that's hard to do. When that happens, the key is finding ways to accept them as they are, and work with the power of your thoughts to influence a better outcome. Your thoughts are more powerful than you realize. They create what you experience in your life. Eventually, a difference between you and someone else is going to be big enough to make you feel upset. Instead of suffering though that, or lashing out in anger, there are things you can do to calm the waters within yourself, build a bridge across the differences, and create a better situation. You can strengthen your ability to handle differences, navigate through them easily, increase your comfort level with them no matter how different or unreasonable other people might be, and decide to use difference constructively.

Using the universal, practical and spiritual principles in this book, you can claim your own power to create peace in your world—and beyond.

EXPRESSIONS OF GRATITUDE

WITH DEEPEST GRATITUDE, I ACKNOWLEDGE, ABOVE ALL ELSE, THE ONE LIFE and Source - for life itself and its abundant gifts.

So many people have touched my life in meaningful ways, and given me support and encouragement along the way, thus helping me to midwife this book. I wish to thank some of these people here.

Justin Sachs, for publishing my work, and Lauren Milne, for providing editing clarity through keen insights and feedback, and the supportive team of kind souls at Motivational Press, for all the wonderful help and guidance.

Lew Bayer, for your friendship and trust, and for being a living example of honor and integrity in all you say and do. Thank you for facilitating the many opportunities which have led me here.

Tim, my husband, partner and friend, I offer heartfelt gratitude for quietly and steadfastly being there for me, taking care of the foundation on which our family can grow and thrive, and loving me so well – all of which made the creation of this book possible. Thank you for the blessing of your love, and for sharing this lifetime with me.

My four beautiful children, with deep gratitude, for patiently listening to me clarify countless ideas and concepts, and finally, your patience and understanding as I produced this book. Connor, Cassie, Laura and Liam, thank you for being my best teachers in life; your very being inspires me. I love each of you more than words could ever say.

Dad and Mum, sincere gratitude I have for you, for generously and unfailingly giving the best you had to give, right from the beginning. Thank you for giving me life, and for your love, care, and guidance.

Thank you for providing the soil from which my deepest growth emerged, making the writing of this book possible.

Barb and Alex, thank you for the special companionship and support only shared sisterhood can bring, and for the many years shared together, loving, learning, and growing. You have each contributed by walking your own path with integrity, and thus inspiring and encouraging me to do the same.

Jodi, Barb, Rita and Shari, my deepest gratitude for the blessing of your friendship, for holding the light through our souls` journey from the beginning, and for providing loving space to help the birthing of the book take place.

Leo Sawicki, I am grateful to you for holding a candle to light my way, and for demonstrating what true freedom looks like.

Jennifer Ferguson, thank you for your unconditional friendship and support, and interest in the creation of this book. Your honesty and integrity are true beacons of goodness in this world.

Bob Houston, thank you for your encouragement and support along the way, for sharing happy memories, and for always welcoming me back "home".

Mom and Dad Desautels, thank you so very much for your gentle support of me and my family, and always demonstrating true kindness.

Mariette Jessup, thank you so much for encouraging me to stay the course, and for your understanding of "writer world".

VIVE LA DIFFERENCE!

EVERYBODY IS DIFFERENT. SOMETIMES, THOUGH, PEOPLE ARE *VERY* DIFFERENT from us. Sometimes these differences, whether in culture, opinion, or anything at all, make us feel angry or upset. You know it when you deeply disagree with them, or you cannot stand to be around them for whatever reason. Maybe you resent what they've done in the past. The difference between you and them feels really unpleasant, and often conflict ensues. Recently, at one of my daughter's soccer games, the coach of the opposing team was pacing up and down the sidelines, shouting instructions, flailing his arms, jumping up and down when the referee made calls against his team, and making a big scene during the whole game. He encouraged his players to hit, to fake injury... anything to get ahead. He was obstreperous and outrageous. The parents on our team were affronted by his behavior, and felt upset that he was carrying on so. One commented that the coach was going to give himself a heart attack. Another said she was going to bolt across the field and give him a piece of her mind—or fist, whichever felt right in the moment. All the parents of our team were furious. This coach had a passionate style, a complete devotion to the result he wanted, and pursued that single-mindedly, to the exclusion of all else. He simply didn't care what we thought. The difference between his approach and ours was palpable, and the result was....anger. Had the game not ended when it did, a yelling match would have occurred.

Differences create adversity, which we think we'd rather live without. Frankly, things that are different from us make us uncomfortable and, if the difference is big enough, we feel negative emotion. We all have different thresholds for the moment at which we become uncomfortable (some are more easygoing than others, for example), but eventually, everyone experiences discomfort (like feeling upset or angry) because of differences with others. When we differ from others (enough to get angry, for example), we encounter adversity. This is not only normal, but should be celebrated—this is actually the very creative tension we want to work with!

Adversity—which springs from diversity—is actually our friend. It doesn't matter if it comes in the form of annoying people, challenging life situations, or impossible circumstances. Without it, there is no creative tension, no excitement, no interest, and no fun. We need adversity; it is the creative clay we work with as we navigate everyday life. We use it to shape our lives and the world around us. It makes life fun and exciting, even if it demands that we deal with annoying people, or face the myriad personal equivalents of unexpected hairpin turns in the road, dangerous white water rapids, and dizzyingly dangerous falls. Difference is a force for change and creativity. It demands something from us, and asks that we choose a response. We can accept it, adapt to it, ignore it, or push against it. We can choose our response deliberately, or reach for the selection of automatic responses we've become used to in the past. Regardless of how we respond to it, it *is*. Without it, we would not be galvanized into adapting or changing anything. It generates the impetus for reevaluation and new approaches. Creativity spirals outward from every perceived and manifested difference.

Since difference *is*, and since it's such wonderful creative "clay," it makes sense to make friends with it. The first step in making friends with our differences with others is recognizing the life-giving value of adversity. The next step is allowing people to be as they are. It's futile to complain about or "push against" situations or people, wishing they were different than they are. We do this all the time, of course: we complain about and criticize people, even though we know it won't change anything. Maybe we're secretly hoping they'll just stop being the way they are and be more like...us! Nonetheless, there is wisdom and power in recognizing that you need to work with the materials you have. Allowing and even embracing *what is* is quite simple. It involves being in the present moment, listening to others, and thinking critically about the stories we tell ourselves. Then we need to understand the power of our thoughts *and* that we can direct them as we choose, and thereby influence the result. Being in the present moment helps us set aside our thinking, which is usually frenetic, habitual, repetitive, and negative. And when we are actively thinking, we want to do so deliberately, and allow for new possibilities to emerge in any situation.

Allowing for dissimilarities (the open acceptance of people and things as they are) clears our minds, builds goodwill, builds bridges over the things that divide us, and conserves energy. From this strong foundation we can guide our thoughts and attitudes in a productive way toward outcomes that we prefer. It's important to understand that we each have creative power to influence our world through thought and feeling, and that we can guide this power consciously. When we recognize the power we have within us, we can embrace difference and adversity without fear, knowing that we can really make a difference for the better in our lives. This inner work makes us effective in our outer work.

Essentially, allowing people to be as they are *conserves* energy, and using our attention and attitude on purpose *directs* energy. We aim, in our acceptance of others and in conscious choices in our thinking, to say yes rather than no to others and their differences with us.

Difference is creative. It generates motion. While it is open to us to handle our differences the way we always have, we cannot access the power of difference with habitual ways of thinking. In fact, difference *removes* our power if we resist what is, and if we are not aware of our thoughts and emotions or using them on purpose. Accessing the power of difference requires that we change some mental patterns.

I am very general in my references to culture and cultural differences, when I mention them. This is because our inner dynamics are the same regardless of the nature of the difference between people. The nature of the difference is irrelevant. How we feel in response to the difference is everything. *This book is designed to help you in navigating interpersonal differences whether you are living through conflict at work, in your family, with your neighbors, or between cultures.* Cultural differences tend to touch us more deeply and can therefore appear more pronounced, so they are an integral aspect of the content of this book. I have taken the liberty of speaking about "Western" cultures, about Greek culture, about female versus male culture, etc. These categories are not academically correct, and are too general to be of any use in that framework. They are colloquial and imprecise. I use them because they are understandable without inviting a lot of qualification and explanation. Again, I use them because, ultimately, they are irrelevant. The focus for the book is our discomfort with difference—in other words, our emotions, which flow from our thoughts—regardless of how precisely or properly that difference is defined. The difference itself matters less for the purposes of this book than does the discomfort we feel because of the difference. In other words, the *discomfort* is relevant, not the difference.

And indeed, this is eventually the place we come to when we speak about cultural difference: eventually, there will be a difference in interpretation of what's "best," which throws us into a quagmire of "either/or." This occurs between people, spouses, companies, countries, and cultures. There is more fear in the public consciousness this decade about cultural difference—particularly with respect to religious difference and terrorism. If we can recognize the fears we have about difference and claim our personal power through awareness and new skills, we can facilitate change on a global scale. And while it's true that generalized fear has become palpable, there is also a commensurate worldwide effort at the grassroots level to reach out and bridge differences between people and communities to foster inclusiveness. This book tells another story—we can work *around* either/or. We need not be trapped into dueling cultures or perspectives on any issue or in any situation. But this takes a reconceptualizing of how we ordinarily see the world.

SEPARATE AND APART?

IT LOOKS LIKE YOU AND I ARE SEPARATE. IT LOOKS LIKE ALL THE OBJECTS IN this room, including the people, are separate, solid entities. However, when we observe each of these things through a microscope we see they are not exactly as they appear. They are made up of millions of molecules. If we observe more deeply still we understand that the molecular world gives way to atoms, then again to the subatomic reality in which we now know we—and all "physical" objects—are actually clouds of information and energy. Interestingly, there is no difference at all between the energy cloud that is a human being and the tree outside the window, except the rate at which their energy patterns vibrate. Both are made of the same "stuff," and neither is inherently separate from the other. There is in fact nothing solid about us, or the world around us, at all. Science helped us with this new way of seeing; it expanded our horizons of understanding so we could view the world in a new way.

More importantly, do we *feel* separate? In 1914, despite the heavy fighting, death, and casualties in the World War I trenches, when Christmas Day arrived at Ploegsteert, Belgium, German and British soldiers (bitter enemies) honored each other with handshakes, gifts, and shared food in the famous Christmas Truce. This was a connection of joy and goodwill which was felt perhaps to be larger than each of them individually and larger than the political causes they fought for. There opened the possibility of connection.[1]

Have you ever seen a conflict brewing, only to witness it dissipate when something unexpected happens? Years ago, a union picket line blocked the front of a local liquor store. It was a hot summer day, and customers wanted cold beer to stave off the heat. But to get the beer, they had to cross the picket line, which resulted in an exchange

---

[1] Quote from a letter written by British Lt. M.S. Richardson to his family in Wakefield, Alan, Christmas in the Trenches. (Stroud, United Kingdom: The History Press Ltd. 2006)

of angry insults. A crowd had gathered, sensing the impending conflict. Suddenly, a child riding by on a bike slipped on some gravel in the parking lot and fell. Everyone nearby rushed to help the child, who was crying and bloody. Within minutes, the very individuals who were prepared to fight about their differences in front of the liquor store were working together to help the little boy, and after emergency crews arrived to take over, had become friends. They shook hands and wished each other well. At the outset, they felt separate because of their difference of opinion, but just one event bound them together for a common purpose. The feeling of separation vanished.

We can allow the Other, whether it is a person or a culture, to be as they are, and allow the situation and moment we are in to be as it is. There is no need to worry about it, complain about it, or fight against it.

In doing this, we surrender all resistance to things or people being the way they are and believing the things they do. We fully accept, so we are free to work with the materials we actually have—the situation itself, plus the materials within our own personal control: our attention and our attitude. We work with the power of our thoughts. This is where our power lives: in the nonresistant moment, the moment in which we are thinking and feeling and experiencing. We can focus on things we wish to cultivate and remove our attention from things we do not. We can become aware of our attitudes or feelings, and so begin to harness their power and direct them toward ideas we prefer. We focus on and lean toward things we like—toward the best in others, in situations, in differences—thereby influencing their growth.

Moreover, when we accept everything as it is, we are much more powerful. We are not fighting the current—we are embracing the potential within the difference by flowing with the current. By allowing others, we conserve valuable energy. By directing our thoughts and attitudes, we direct our energy in a more focused, efficient, and effective way.

This book is for people who want a better and brighter world, a world in which we can all cocreate and coexist and cooperate. It's about what to do when your personal threshold for tolerating difference is at its limit. If you don't think this applies to you, consider the last time (yesterday? this morning?) you were annoyed with or angry at someone. You navigate interpersonal differences constantly. If you never feel negative emotion as a result of interacting with others, this book is not for you. If, however, you experience negativity once in a while, this book is designed to address that.

Each of us plays a powerful part in shaping this world, and the choices we make create the reality we experience, both individually and collectively.

> *"He who lives in harmony with himself lives in harmony with the universe."*
>
> —*Marcus Aurelius*

DANCING WITH DIFFERENCES

I AM NOT A DANCER. I REALLY DON'T GO OUT MUCH, AND EVEN WHEN I do, it's not to dance. However, I have watched competitive ballroom dancing on TV a few times. The dancers were, of course, beautiful—in appearance, skill, and the way they moved together. It was this latter aspect that intrigued me: separate individuals moving together across the floor as one whole, complete, fluid being. Feminine and masculine, yin and yang, thrusting and yielding, entwined in limbs and breath. They moved as if there was no separation at all between them—as if they were one.

I mentally drew parallels with nature—schools of fish, flocks of birds. The movement of creatures in synchronous harmony, as we see in nature, is so much more than a mechanical process. Birds do not *think* their way into the sky together, nor do schools of fish meet each morning to coordinate their swimming schedules. As I watched the dancers on TV it became clear they were not *thinking* their way through dance steps. Once those steps are learned, another process takes over and is surrendered to. It is guided not by the mind's machinations, but by higher awareness—of which thought is a subset. Perhaps it was the perfection of their orchestrated movements that brought this contrast home to me in the way ordinary differences could not.

Whatever the case, the vision of the dancers became for me a symbol for integrating all differences and all separation between people because each is allowed his or her individuality, and yet we can enjoy and appreciate the difference (the flash of color of the woman's dress against the black of the man's tuxedo, the blending of the yin and the yang, feminine and masculine).

Dancing is celebration—of life, of emotion (even if it's sadness or anger, as is used in some cultures), of physicality.

It is done alone and together; it integrates body, soul, mind, and spirit; it is creative; it allows and celebrates difference.

We can integrate ourselves with the best aspects in others, and we can learn to draw forth from anyone who is "different"—including a loved one with whom we are having an argument—the very best they have to offer through the power of acceptance, focus, and feeling.

To navigate differences of any kind effectively, we need to prepare an inner foundation—to awaken our innate ability to allow others to be who they are, find our inner balance, and consciously direct the power of our thought. And this inner change is reflected in outer circumstances.

LET'S MEET IN THE FIELD

"Beyond right doing and wrong doing there is a field. I will meet you there."

—*Rumi*

RUMI, THE BRILLIANT THIRTEENTH-CENTURY POET, TELLS US THERE IS A PLACE beyond right and wrong—beyond judgement, in other words. He points to a place *beyond* the opposites that we bounce between every day in our waking lives. It says not only that such a place exists, but that we can meet there, beyond the differences we experience as human beings. We are accustomed to sorting people and events in our lives into categories: ones we like, ones we don't, and ones we're not sure about. We talk casually about the weather being "good" or "bad," or current events in the news being "good" or "bad." But what if neither is true?

A young, white, educated, Canadian-born friend of mine travelled and worked abroad in her twenties. She's curious and outgoing, and was remarkably facile in adapting to life in many different countries. Eventually she arrived in Istanbul, met a young Turkish man, fell in love, and married. She lived and worked happily for years in Turkey, undergoing many personal adjustments to fit into the Muslim culture there. Later, the she and her husband moved to Canada. There came a hot summer day when she put on a pair of shorts, and it was then that the marital challenges began in earnest. Each spouse clearly understood they were from different cultures, and even recognized that they were to some extent "products" of their respective cultures. Still, my friend related, "He was really upset that I'd wear that. To him, it was totally wrong for a married woman to dress that way. I told him 'We're in my country now, and this is my culture. Here, women do wear shorts, and that's who I am.' But you know what? Even though we knew about the differences in our cultures, it still came down to: if yours says *this* and mine says *that*, which one is right? Either it's yours or it's mine."

On one level of understanding, there is right and wrong. But Rumi tells us there is something beyond that. That is where true connection lives, that is where peace lives. Imagining that this possibility exists fills our hearts with hope. Can we stretch beyond our ideas of right and wrong to meet in this field? In the "field beyond right and wrong doing," we are not encumbered by concepts. Concepts are products of our minds, and often serve to divide us. Right-doing and wrong-doing are concepts—ideas that are taught to us by other people through culture and tradition. In the "field" beyond these, however, things and people simply *are*. We are not attached to any particular ideas, beliefs, or labels about them. We see *them*, not ideas *about* them.

It is the nature of the mind to automate. Once a thing is seen and experienced, it goes in the mind's "file banks" for easy reference and convenience. But over many years in a human life, all things are catalogued this way. Eventually, we turn not to the thing itself but to the mind's files—pictures from the past that never *know* a thing, only *about* it. And we move further and further away from the purity of the thing itself until it becomes gray and lifeless, as if it is printed in ink in a catalogue.

Our minds do not have the capacity to really know a thing or a person at all. A mind cannot know beauty, for example. It can only know *about* beauty. This is a very important, yet very subtle distinction. To know beauty is to feel it within your own being—to receive it there, to apprehend it in its essence. Notice how formless this attempt at description is. Your mind might feel annoyed with it because the mind only works in forms—including abstract forms like ideas and concepts, beliefs and judgements. It makes them all into things. But beauty, love—these can't be things, so the mind has little to say other than lists of qualities *about* them.

The brilliance of the mind to capture stills and catalogue them knows no bounds. It sorts, typecasts, arranges, speculates, compares, and analyzes. And its brilliance, untamed, is a kind of death to all things. That life in a flower, which speaks of eternity; that scent of a flower, which wraps the soul in heaven; that color of a flower, which lifts the heart, dances away from the mind's machinations, light as a wisp on the wind. Its beauty simply cannot be captured and held.

But we can behold the flower, in silence, and set down the mind. In so doing, the flower opens itself to you. Then you can know the flower as a whole, in its beauty and full being, which is so much more than simply knowing things about it. And maybe you can be content with an empty page in the catalogue where "Flower" might have been. You have received its most treasured gift, which cannot be borne by a page in a book. Its beauty and essence can only be given in the moment, and will inevitably pass away. Do not chase it, but know it has become part of you, and now lives in the words you speak and the thoughts you think and the way you live in this world.

If you are able to walk past, even for a moment, the ideas you have *about* someone or their culture, you can see these people more clearly and allow them to be as they are. You can apprehend their be-ing, instead of just regarding them as a collection of concepts. You then can let go of the need to judge them (are they right? are they wrong?) and instead let them be, and let the differences between you be. This opens up inner space to let the possibility of a field *beyond* right and wrong be also. There is indeed a place beyond the duality of judgements where things simply *are*. This is the place where we are not separate. This is the place that bridges all perceived differences. Apply it to directing your thoughts and intentions toward better outcomes.

Goodwill toward Men

"Goodwill toward men" is easy when the wine is flowing, the money is plentiful, and the sun is shining. It's easy to generously bestow kind thoughts on others, give the benefit of the doubt, and "live and let live." We easily recognize the humanity of others. We love the idea of diversity. We love the idea of inclusion in our schools, workplaces, and countries, and the idea of embracing difference. Many countries aspire to this, and it is reflected in their legislation, business organizations, and government agencies. Vive la Difference!

In the midst of deep differences, however, it's a bit more challenging to hold charitable views of others. Sometimes the difference is too big, or too close to our hearts, or too threatening to who we are. When that happens, we feel annoyed, angry, defensive, or disgusted. We react in a number of different ways: we usually put up fences, defend, close ranks, shut down, start petitions, or lash out verbally or physically.

What do you do when you have to deal with someone who says or does offensive things? Or who refuses to be reasonable? What if you need to work together with someone whose ideas, habits, religion, attitudes, or mannerisms you disagree with or disapprove of? What if you are in a relationship with someone who acts stubborn or is inconsiderate? The deeper the difference, the more we notice the "otherness" in the Other. Have you ever noticed that when someone cuts you off in traffic, or pushes past you in a line, or is rude to you, the qualities (real or imagined) that make them different than you emerge sharply? The things that bother us about others emerge in our minds when we are uncomfortable or annoyed, and they become barriers between us. Where just moments ago we were blissfully imagining peace on earth and goodwill to men, something annoying occurs and we notice how "other" the other person is. We just want them to behave better, be better, follow the rules, be nicer, give more, stop doing the things that bother us. We feel that if they would just be different from the way they are, the world would be a better place, and we could feel better about things and get on with life.

Rob, a prominent lawyer, took his client Saul out for lunch in celebration of a successful settlement of Saul's litigation file. During lunch they spoke of many things. At one point, Rob explained how important it was, in his view, for children to be involved in a religious faith from an early age. Saul, on the other hand, disagreed, feeling that decisions about faith must wait until a child reaches what he called the "age of reason." Both men were fathers of young children, both felt passionately about their ideas, and both thought that the other was doing a disservice to his children. The remainder of their visit was strained.

Clodagh is from Ireland, where a child's first communion, especially for girls, is akin to a wedding—a huge event involving expensive gowns, photographers, and the like. She is planning her daughter's first communion in typical Irish style, and has invited family and friends from all over the world. She heard about a comment made by a friend that the celebration was inappropriately excessive and lavish; the friend thought such an event was totally out of proportion for a first communion, which, in her eyes, ought to be quiet and simple. Clodagh was deeply insulted. To her, the splendor of the event signified her family's joy. The friend's disapproval stung, and a rift in the friendship began.

At some point, everyone becomes uncomfortable with difference. Interestingly, the nature of the difference between people matters very little. The difference between people could be about the best interpretation of religious scripture, how to raise children, where the community library should be built, how to show respect to people, how to best protect the environment, how to behave, things we should or shouldn't do—anything at all.

The simple *existence* of the discomfort is what is important. Discomfort means feeling annoyed, angry, impatient, fearful, worried, anxious, or even hateful. Unpleasant emotions flow directly from thoughts, and it is the orchestration of the two that creates barriers in our relationships with others. We can analyze any problem until the proverbial cows come home, but this will not address the *real* problem, which is the discomfort itself. We try to alleviate the discomfort, make the bad feelings go away, and thus make ourselves feel better, but it is a surface effort and does not get at the root of the issue. Have you found yourself feeling increasingly irritated by someone who does the same old annoying thing, over and over, and then you just blew up at them? Like a boiling kettle, the pressure in you rises until it blows off steam. The pressure in the kettle increases as energy builds, and the dynamics are the same in you. The energy of anger becomes larger until you are compelled to discharge it. It feels better, in the moment, to release that awful pressure by stomping, throwing, or yelling. It does make the anger go away—temporarily. The root of the matter, however, is your thought about the annoying person. How we feel is caused by how we think. The *thought* is the cause, not the person.

Sometimes it's hard to know exactly what we feel. Generally speaking, we are not accustomed to paying attention to this. A wonderful life coach I know, when she asks a new client what they are feeling in that moment, says in every single case the person looks stunned. They have the classic deer-caught-in-the-headlights kind of stare. It takes them several seconds to connect with, and then identify, the emotional state they are in. Many people are unable to even do this. In any event, when we aren't sure how we're feeling, our behavior can provide clues: we might act nervous, disgusted, aggressive, or judgemental. When we dislike something, it's because something is causing us discomfort, even if it's an emotion we cannot identify precisely. Sometimes we just get a bad feeling. We experience varying levels of discomfort with difference—we can have dramatic anger during an argument, or just a low-level unease or distaste about someone's personal habits or demeanor, for example.

It is the discomfort about difference, fed by our thoughts, that guides our choices and actions. Each of us has our own personal "discomfort threshold" depending on the situation, the issue, and even what mood we're in. The primary issue with cultural diversity, for example, is people's discomfort with difference. Cultural differences are a *type* of difference we experience. There is no real distinction between a cultural difference and a difference of opinion—the feelings and reactions we have are the same. It does not matter what the difference is; the issue—discomfort with difference—is the same. Cultural differences are top of mind now, given the world climate regarding immigration, politics, racism, and extremism. But they are not different than any other kind of difference, perhaps with one exception: they go very deeply into who we are as human beings. For that reason, they activate strong emotions and thus are more volatile. So what we are really looking for is a way of creating a new set of responses to things.

Understanding the specific nature of differences between people and cultures is helpful, to be sure. Armed with more knowledge, we can communicate more easily, and to some extent rationalize why beliefs and behaviors are the way they are. But people, cultures, and the differences between them continually evolve. It's a moving target. We tend to spend time and energy analyzing the differences and how we respond to them. But the real issue is our discomfort because our emotions, fed by our thoughts, guide our words and actions. It's the *discomfort* of difference we need to explore and develop a new relationship with.

The Beauty of Adversity

Every story ever told has, wound within its pages, a tale of adversity. Adversity is life-giving. When things go wrong, the plot gets interesting. We have a chance to sharpen our wits or swords on a difficult set of circumstances. We get to play with different ideas of who we are, test our strengths, and demonstrate our ideas and beliefs through action.

For instance, in the *Minecraft* game, players can create a personal "world" in which they can choose either to have everything perfect from the start (creative mode) or to have to create everything they need to survive (survival mode). In creative mode, a player is virtually invincible: resources are unlimited, you don't need food, and you can even fly. You can make anything you wish, out of any material you like, easily. You simply select what you want and, voila!

In survival mode, by contrast, you start with nothing—you collect wood, find and fashion tools (stone ones, wood ones), make a house, hide from bad guys, make torches for light, and eat (to maintain your energy) by fishing, growing wheat, etc. My kids started out playing the game in creative mode. They built towns and palaces in magical worlds out of ice and diamonds. And yet they prefer survival mode over creative, despite the inherent challenges; they appreciate their creations so much more. As adults, we *think* we want creative mode— well-feathered nests, all the money we want, anything at the touch of a button. But survival—creating our own "platform," deciding what we want, choosing our priorities, and experimenting with the options available—this is actually the fun and satisfying part. Stepping back and appreciating a tough job well-done is exhilarating.

Babies face adversity in learning to walk: they struggle to stand, cruise, and take their first steps. Each stage in the process is fraught with challenge and risk. But anyone who has witnessed a baby's first success knows by the joyful expression its radiant pride and satisfaction!

Similarly, without Darth Vader, would Luke Skywalker be a brave Jedi knight? His growth, challenges, and excitement are borne of the adversity, the play of light against dark. How would he know himself to be the brave knight he dreams of being without an evil empire to test himself against?

If all the characters in fairy tales were kind and fair, there'd be no creative tension. If Snow White lived in creative mode, she'd have met Prince Charming and sailed off into the sunset immediately. But their happily-ever-after ending is so much more delicious *because* she survives a murder attempt, getting lost in the dark woods, making friends of the dwarfs, fearing the evil Queen, eating the poisoned apple, and falling into a near-fatal coma.

Adversity plays the same role in your life. If you have ever signed up for a white water river raft expedition, you sign up because it's going to be fun. Why is it fun? Because the white water is dangerous. It is an adverse condition that you can experience and "overcome," thereby experiencing the exhilaration of...well, being alive. Therein lies its fun. When our lives are smooth and uneventful, our contentment is short-lived. If you signed up for the white water river trip and told the guide you wanted to skip the hard stuff and just join the group at the end you'd look a bit silly. And yet, this is what we secretly feel when adversity shows up. We complain, we wish we didn't have to deal with it, we shrink from the idea of dealing with hassles. Yet hassles, mountains to climb, and things going wrong are the very things we extract our inner riches from. Most movies are based on things going "wrong." We really do want the river ride after all. Without it, our lives become flat and dull. After all, how interesting would life be if you were surrounded by people who agreed with everything you thought and said one hundred percent of the time?

Adversity flows naturally from diversity. Difference brings interest, excitement, surprise, and challenge. Every time.

After all, what *is* the light without the dark? It has no meaning. It is only after we meet the dark, with its shadows and unknowns, that we appreciate the gifts the light brings.

MANY WORLDS

I GOT HIRED AS A PART-TIME BAKERY SALES CLERK WHILE I WAS ATTENDING university. From the moment I began, I knew I had entered a foreign land. I was twenty years younger than the other employees, and hadn't a clue. They bustled about, filling shelves and rotating product, slicing bread and packaging buns, decorating cakes and waiting on customers. The kindest among them regarded me with patient condescension as she instructed me, for the tenth time, on the self-evident process of rotating bread: oldest to the front, freshest to the back. One day, they discovered moldy bread that I'd forgotten to remove from the shelf. The senior clerk said, "HOW can you be in University and not get this, Janet? Where is your common sense?" Newer employees than me seemed to know what to do and how to prioritize their tasks.

I never did get the hang of it, but I did recognize the bakery was a world unto itself. Cake decorating was ranked highest, and you sought to do that in your future. You'd really arrived if you got the chance to do that. The bread slicer, who had the earliest shift other than the bakers, was next most important. Your status and respect among bakery peers depended on your ability to work efficiently, slice bread evenly and neatly, and handle all cleaning tasks with swift dispatch. I was really good at interacting with customers. I always made them smile, and was very accommodating. But this counted for little, as it didn't "get the job done" quickly. Eventually they threw up their hands, deemed me hopeless, and transferred me to another store, hoping that manager could do something with me.

Later, I worked as a server (then called a waitress) at a local pub. That pub was its own world, too. There, speed was crucial as well, but so was the ability to carry your tray the "right" way and to hold all the customers' orders in your head. In that world, you agreed with the fiery, temperamental cook and took care not to upset him. The regulars had certain days they'd prefer to come, had their favorite tables, and always had the same drinks. If these regulars liked you, you could take afternoon bar shifts. You knew which one was recovering from an operation, which had a new grandchild, and all the ups and downs of their lives.

In the suburban minor hockey world, a deep camaraderie exists among the long-suffering, exhausted parents of young players. In that world, devotion to your children is shown by your faithful attendance and attention at all games and practices, involvement in tournaments, and arrangement of the family schedule around hockey. Respect naturally flows to parents with multiple hockey players—the greater the imagined sacrifice, the greater the respect given.

I had a friend who was a second-generation Italian from Eastern Canada. I spent a lot of time with her and her family. In their world, family and food were everything. They cooked everything from scratch, ironed with starch, fitted their toddlers with "proper" leather walking shoes, and took great care in preparing their meals (always the freshest ingredients, nothing less would do) and in living well. One never took shortcuts in quality of living. My friend had never eaten packaged macaroni and cheese until she met me; even then, I think she tried it only to indulge me. Sunday morning walks with the family and a stop at Starbucks were de rigueur. In that world, you lived well and took care of your family and friends; loyalty was valued and expected, as was honoring all birthdays and life celebrations in the whole extended family.

Have you ever heard anyone say, "she's in her own world" or "he's in his own world"? They are quite correct, only it actually applies to everyone.

Every person, place, group, and family is a world—a community—with its own language and symbols, expectations and roles, challenges and victories. Each world has a mood, tone, flavor, and worldview. Each one values different things, and what they value defines who they are as a community.

I am a world unto myself: I have thoughts, a personal history, values, genes, a body, personality, emotions, tendencies, etc. I am mind, body, and spirit. My blood cells are part of the world of my body's circulatory system; my immune system is a world, as is my neurological system, and my limbic system. There are many different layers and components and subcomponents to each of these worlds, each comprising a smaller community/world. Every person is made of many worlds, and exists in many more worlds again—family and culture, for example—and like the physical system, each of these can exist in harmony with the others. There is a great difference between the muscular system and the endocrine system, for example, but each system *allows the other to be what it is*, and *finds ways to operate in harmony*. The successful coexistence of all the body's systems looks like a pluralistic society. There is an underlying harmony beneath the differences.

When, for example, we deepen our vision of the environment around us—observing objects as solid at first, then bringing out microscopes to see deeper, and then deeper still, by delving into the atomic and then subatomic realms—moving from Newtonian principles of physics to quantum ideas, we see that these worlds, while different, are complementary. I am, after all, my molecules, and atoms, and all the space in between them. They are all "true," just different levels of the same thing. Each is valid, and yet is a different aspect of the whole.

Every person lives in many worlds. And every aspect of you is a potential difference—and similarity—with someone else. There are infinite ways to see the world, and yet each human being exists in many different overlapping "worlds." Our worlds are akin to cultures; each world we occupy has its own people and way of seeing things. Your workplace, stage of life, gender, favorite sport, city, region, faith community, education level—all contain within them, generally speaking, a shared perspective. Think about how many worlds you occupy: your family, school, work, community, interests, hobbies, organizations. Include all the worlds you were part of in the past. Notice the interface between each world and its adjacent worlds? Notice they are different and yet in some fashion complementary?

The worlds you live in shape your perspective, and perspective is everything.

There was once a stonecutter who was dissatisfied with himself and his life. One day, he passed a wealthy merchant's house. He looked through the window as he passed by and saw many beautiful things: fine fabrics and art, servants and crystal goblets overflowing with wine. "How powerful that merchant must be!" thought the stonecutter. He became very envious and wished that he could be like the merchant. To his great surprise, he suddenly became the merchant, enjoying more luxuries and power than he had ever imagined, but envied and detested by those less wealthy than himself. Soon, a high official passed by, carried in a sedan chair, accompanied by attendants and escorted by soldiers. Everyone, no matter how wealthy, had to bow low before the procession. "How powerful that official is!" he thought. "I wish that I could be a high official!" Suddenly, he became the high official, carried everywhere in his embroidered sedan chair, feared and hated by people everywhere. It was a hot summer day, so the official felt very uncomfortable in the sticky sedan chair. He looked up at the sun. It shone proudly in the sky, unaffected by his presence. "How powerful the sun is!" he thought. "I wish that I could be the sun!"

Suddenly, he became the sun, shining fiercely down on everyone, scorching the fields, cursed by the farmers and laborers. Then a huge black cloud moved between him and the earth, so that his light could no longer shine on everything below. "How powerful that storm cloud is!" he thought. "I wish that I could be a cloud!" Then he became the cloud, flooding the fields and villages, shouted at by everyone. But soon he found that he was being pushed away by some great force, and realized that it was the wind. "How powerful it is!" he thought. "I wish that I could be the wind!"

Then he became the wind, blowing tiles off the roofs of houses, uprooting trees, feared and hated by all below him. But after a while, he ran up against something that would not move, no matter how forcefully he blew against it—a huge, towering rock. "How powerful that rock is!" he thought. "I wish that I could be a rock!"

Then he became the rock, more powerful than anything else on earth. But as he stood there, he heard the sound of a hammer pounding a chisel into the hard surface, and felt himself being changed. "What could be more powerful than I, the rock?" he thought. He looked down and saw far below him the figure of a stonecutter.

The man experienced all these different, and yet related, perspectives on life. And the worlds you occupy serve a similar function. Recognizing this enables us to appreciate the range and relativity of our own experiences—and thus enables us to be more capable of borrowing other perspectives too, to foster greater understanding between worlds. [2]

My friend is an RCMP (Royal Canadian Mounted Police) officer in

---

2 Reps, Paul, and Nyogen, Senzaki, Contributor, *Zen Flesh and Zen Bones*. (North Clarendon, VT, 2008: Tuttle Publishing)

northern Canada. One night she took me on a "ride-along" with her in the police vehicle. I walked with her into seedy bars, back alleys, and tough neighborhoods, all the while keeping an eye out for particular troublemakers, observing who was hanging around with whom, who was and wasn't following their bail conditions. What looked to me like an ordinary bar was suddenly transformed, through borrowing my friend's perspective, into a threatening place filled with dangerous shadows and intrigue. As she explained the kinds of things police look for when they walk the "beat," I was able to borrow her perspective for a time and look through her eyes at the world; it was dark, dangerous, and full of threats, and because of that, it was exciting. Suddenly, I did notice the gleam of a knife in the back pocket of a tough-looking guy at the pool table. They'd been watching him for some time, as he was out on bail for an assault charge.

We visited the jail cells at the police station; a bored officer processing paperwork on the latest case barely looked up as we brought in a new one. We drove to Tim Hortons, where we had a lively visit with fellow officers sharing tales of what had happened in the streets so far that night. In the police world, camaraderie was crucial: they needed humor, bonding, and trust between them. They were a team of protectors, relying on each other and watching each other's backs in a frequently thankless role.

I could borrow my friend's perspective by experiencing her world on this ride-along, and I thus expanded my own perspective. I could then recognize how the police world intersected with my own worlds in a complementary way—I could appreciate the differences and allow them to coexist. I can safely carry on with my regular activities each day (driving, working, shopping, socializing) now aware of the role the police play, and the undercurrents that swirl beneath apparently calm surfaces, knowing there are benevolent forces at work taking care of threats that I, as an ordinary citizen, cannot practically handle on my own. By understanding her world, I could see how her work made possible my safe passage through everyday life, and thus truly appreciate it.

THE OTHER

"That same choice our ancestors faced thousands of years ago faces us today as well, with undiminished intensity—a choice as fundamental and categorical as it was back then. How should we act toward Others?" [3]

—*Ryszard Kapuscinski*

ENCOUNTERS WITH OTHERS ARE A FACT OF LIFE FOR HUMAN BEINGS. HOW WE decide to act in these encounters determines whether those encounters lead to violence or to cooperation, to bridge building or to the building of walls. Our fear and dislike of the Other, of which there are so many examples past and present, arises because of difference—specifically, our discomfort with difference. The Other brings difference right to our doorstep: change from the known, things we are not used to, things we are afraid of and insecure about, things we judge as bad, even things we regard as repugnant or inappropriate, etc. In many countries, immigrants are regarded with fear and suspicion; they are different, smell funny, eat the wrong foods in the wrong way, don't talk or act like "us," and their arrival somehow means there is less for the rest of us and things will never be the same.

When we meet others who are different than us, it's commonplace to end up in a duel, conflict, or war. Human history is brimming with

---

3 Kapuscinski, Ryszard, *Encountering the Other: The Challenge for the 21st Century*, New perspectives Quarterly, vol. 22 #4 (2005)

such examples, marked by countless battlefields and ruins scattered around the world. Another strategy is common: to segregate ourselves by creating barriers between Us and Them (to keep Us in and, more importantly, Them out). The Great Wall of China, the towers and gates of Babylon, and the Incan stone walls are examples of this. When we don't like someone for whatever reason, we tend to put up personal barriers like invisible "fences" and retreat behind them. We also have the choice to open to Them, and meet to exchange thoughts, and ideas, thereby discovering shared experiences, visions, and values. The historical Silk Road and Amber Route stand as such reminders of human accomplishment in cooperation and mutual acceptance of differences. "The Other" in those cases did not equate to "foreignness" and "danger," but "new possibilities" instead. If you can see yourself in the Other, even a little, then it's simple to find a bridge across differences. Basic recognition of our shared humanity makes cooperation and respect possible.

Cultural Differences: One Difference to Rule Them All

CULTURE DEEPLY INFLUENCES EACH OF US. IT GIVES US AN IDENTITY AND sense of belonging in the world. Our culture provides the framework to help us understand and interpret the world around us. Culture appears not to be inborn, but learned. A baby is born into the cultures of its family, community, faith tradition, and nation—into a ring of concentric circles, each of which is a culture, or "world"—and absorbs through a combination of "osmosis" and deliberate instruction how to survive; what beauty means; how to love; what to wear; who to speak to, and how, and when; when to stand up and sit down; when to laugh; when to cry; and what to believe about reality. The child learns its culture's stories and wisdom, borne of the culture's journey through time. Every piece of information about surviving and thriving in life is transmitted via culture. My son's long-suffering kindergarten teacher demonstrates every day the sheer volume of information required to "civilize" rambunctious five year olds and prepare them for social intercourse. We don't eat Play Doh, throw toys, push, or punch. We line up, take turns, use the toilet, and wash our hands. We play nice with others (share, regulate our emotions, respect personal space, empathize), follow instructions, and color inside the lines. Embedded within all this complex information are cultural values and assumptions about the world and one's place within it.

Culture is a rich and wonderful set of ideas about absolutely every-thing. It is shared; it's how humans define a common way of being for members of a group. Culture *bestows belonging*. We are by nature so-cial beings, and culture is the means through which we are socialized. It's the way we understand ourselves to be part of something greater than ourselves. Can you think of a time when you were thrilled to be singing your national anthem or celebrating a favorite team's victo-ry—when you were proud of belonging to that? This is the strength of culture and the belonging it gives us. Yet there may be much more depth to the feeling of belonging than we realize. A culture often ex-periences unity because of tragedies in its past.

While it is true that cultural ideas, traditions, and ways of being are learned, this does not preclude a spiritual dimension to the bond amongst the people, nor does it mean that we can take such a bond lightly. Indeed, it has great meaning, and brings depth and richness to people's lives. There is an indefinable dimension to the connection one has to culture—what is it that stirs the blood within the collective breast? What, for example, is that inexplicable "something" that brings tears to my own eyes when I hear the bagpipes of Scotland? Other than a distant ancestral connection, I have no ties in this lifetime to that place. And yet the connection feels as strong and real to me as if I'd personally stood on the legendary Culloden battlefield mourning the dead in 1746.

Often, the ties that bind a culture together are borne of great pain and hardship. Those who cry with you, after all, live in your heart in a way others cannot. Many magnificent cultures around the world are bound together through tears. Together, people survive tragedy and difficulty, yet find solace in caring for and loving each other. The silken cords of love that bind their hearts together, however, are also a protective shield from those "outside" their "family."

Like many cultures around the world, the Acadiens, or Acadians, descendants of French colonists, suffered terrible hardship in the struggle for dominance between colonial powers. The Acadian story began in what is now maritime Canada. During the Great Deportation beginning in 1755, these people were forcibly expelled from their settled lands and deported to Britain or France, from which they eventually migrated to many places around the world. Thousands of them suffered imprisonment or perished through disease or drowning on the long voyages. Poems, stories, movies, and songs now carry the story and its memories into the present day; the pain and loss of their shared tragedy is embodied in Longfellow's poem, "Evangeline." [4]Since 1955, every year on August 15, Acadians around the globe gather together in one place for the great Tintamarre to honor those who fought for their survival in the Great Deportation, and celebrate with each other in their accomplishments as a community. My friend Jeanne is Acadian, and has shared with me that she feels a deep longing to be amongst other Acadians, especially near the fifteenth of August. She told me, "I would say it's like a primitive need that runs deep in our veins—just as birds migrate south every year, Acadians are driven to congregate as well."

This sentiment is true for many people, in the context of their own cultural backgrounds.

---

4   Marsh, James H., *The Deportation of the Acadians* (April, 2013) http://www.thecanadianen-cyclopedia.ca/en/article/the-deportation-of-the-acadians-feature/

So, culture unites us and divides us: we unite with others in a group through shared history with its members, and we differentiate ourselves from outsiders the same way. What is important for our purposes is: can we accept others, who live "outside" our cultures, for example, as they are? If the answer is yes, then culture is not a barrier between us. If we cannot, we might look to our culture for the reason. When cultural differences divide us, we find it hard to understand or relate to others outside our own culture, which causes conflict at work, in our communities, and around the world.

We are seldom aware we are seeing everything through a cultural perspective. This is because we are taught this perspective from early infancy, and have no other frame of reference. To a fish living in the water, for example, it's obvious how things are and should be. Everyone has gills, and everyone swims. The fish is not aware of any world outside its own—so it could not conceive of air, other types of beings, or even other bodies of water. Imagine asking the fish, "What is your cultural perspective?" If it could, the fish would laugh and think you were insane. Your question would seem nonsensical. Yet often, we are completely unconscious that we are biased toward others, or biased in our worldview. We like to think we are accepting of others, and of other cultures, and of other ways of doing things, but in reality, we harbor unseen and unrecognized biases that we overlook, and these cause us problems. *We have automatic ways of doing and thinking that we aren't awake to.* A wonderful workshop exercise created by Kimberly Pineda in Building Cultural Competence (2012) explores the nature of what is "obvious" in peeling a banana: your culture teaches you what end of the banana is the "top," and when you learn that, you peel the banana from that place every time. When you observe someone doing it differently, it's surprising because we tend to assume others do things the same way we do. Two people of the same sex holding hands in public, for example, especially if they are men, is deeply uncomfortable for many in Western culture. Many people where I live think it is "obvious" that men don't do that; the appropriate male gestures to show friendship include a handshake, or a clap on the back perhaps. How do you feel about someone who slurps while they eat? How do you feel about someone who does not make eye contact with you when you speak to them? Each of these scenarios could be a cultural difference, depending on the situation, and your reaction to each demonstrates your (automatic) bias. See this as neutral in and of itself. If a reaction is automatic, it is by definition a bias you are not consciously aware of, and if this is so, it hardly makes sense to judge the existence of it. Recognition is the first step—from that point, different choices can be made.

Where I live, Caucasians often ask people with brown skin, "Where are you from?" If they say "Canada" or name a Canadian city or province, they are often asked, "No, where are you FROM?"—meaning, "Where did you emigrate from, or in what country were you born?" Unless a Caucasian has a distinct foreign accent, they are never asked this question. It is assumed they "belong" here, and so no questions are asked. It is a given. Implicit in the question is the assumption that brown-skinned people are not "from" here, and depending on the person asking, hidden within the question could be assumptions—perhaps masking fears—about belonging, about perceptions related to immigration, about scarcity of national resources, etc. Again, we are not judging the existence of bias here. We are simply recognizing that we all have biases, and that we are often unaware that our learned cultural perspectives are fueling them.

If you can recognize you are seeing others and the world *through* the cultural frame of reference you grew up in, it is easier to allow for other views and perspectives, because you would know your way is simply one of many. You become, in other words, less attached to your culture's worldview. If you were travelling and shopping at a crowded marketplace and people were pushing and shoving you to get to the front of a line, or grab items on display, would you be as upset if you knew that that's expected behavior in their culture? Many cultures do not teach children to line up and take turns. And you can also understand that others are seeing you through their cultural frames of reference as well, and you so can allow for that without taking umbrage if they disagree with you in some way.

Understanding that we all look through the lenses of our different cultures leads us quite naturally to a more nonreactive approach, and perhaps enables us to recognize elements of our shared humanity—the things that are universal between us as human beings. We can hold our worldviews more lightly. And if I can see that my culture or worldview is simply one of many and can compare it as such, then perhaps I am much bigger than it is. We can expand past "I am a Canadian" to "I am a human being who lives and works in Canada" to, possibly, "I am a being that is having a human experience at this time." If we can expand our sense of who and what we are, cultural barriers between us will not seem insurmountable, and may in fact be no trouble at all. It is the human mind and its habits of thought that separate us.

Remember the movie *Castaway*? The character, a FedEx employee named Chuck Noland, becomes stranded on an uninhabited island after his plane crashes into the ocean, destroying absolutely everything—his home, his love, his job, his name—every single thing that gave him an identity. Everything that he could possible use to define who "Chuck Noland" is disappears. Imagine that happening to you for a moment. Imagine travelling, getting lost. No money, no ID, no language, no place to stay, no access to a phone, nobody to recognize you. Nobody knows your name. No sense of belonging, no "place" to which you belong. You are now free from all the roles and trappings you understood as your "life." So who are you? Without anyone or anything to reflect your ideas about who you are, how do you define who you are? Without culture or relationships, who are we? Culture is a set of ideas about who we are and how to live; it defines who is "in" and "out" of our group. Creating belonging and separation—barriers to others' belonging—is its nature. Yet it is possible to see beyond the stories we tell about who we are—and who others are.

Castaway shows us that it is possible to exist *outside* the standard ways of defining ourselves. And if that is possible, then it is possible to see beyond the ideas and barriers that divide us.

There is merit in learning about the ways and cultures of others. Expanding our knowledge of other cultures helps us enlarge our perspectives, at least enough to imagine there are others ways of thinking, being, and doing. Considering other points of view helps us recognize that the things we assume are "obvious" are not obvious at all! Should a person consider his family and community first in making a decision, or be accountable to himself and make the decision he personally feels is best? My culture taught me that you're on your own—you need to decide what's best for you and live with that. To me, it's "obvious" that personal fulfillment is the yardstick to use. But in many other cultures, the yardstick to use is the welfare of the family or group.

Cultures are studied and measured along different dimensions of behavior, each dimension being a continuum with opposites at either end.[5] Some cultures are very emotionally expressive, for example, and others are very restrained. Interestingly, this is reflective of the array of differences between individuals, too: while I might be a member of a culture that tends to be expressive, I may be, as an individual within that context, unexpressive. It's helpful and a bit of a relief to learn about the various differences in patterns of being, communicating, and behaving; it helps us understand and put puzzling discrepancies between people(s) into perspective.

Cultures array themselves, much like individuals and families do, along different continuums of behavior. So while the extreme manifestations of each pattern are at either end, there are many "in-be-

---

5 Hofstede, Geert, *Culture's Consequences: Comparing Values, Behaviors, Institutions and Organizations Across Nations*. 2nd Edition, Thousand Oaks CA: Sage Publications, 2001

tween" expressions. (For example, between the qualities of "tall" and "short" , there is a huge array of possibilities: very tall, moderately tall, "normal" height, moderately short, very short, underweight, etc. Further, each of these qualities means something different to the person or culture observing them. "Tall" in one culture or family is not necessarily "tall" in another. So, as a result, it's not fair, really, to generalize about characteristics, as in: "Italians/Germans/Americans are very _____ (fill in the blank)."

It's also important to understand that cultural patterns are only at best loose generalizations. Like any person, I live in many different cultures (my family, my community, my professional groups, my workplace, my country, etc.). My country is Canada: it embraces Western values like individualism, and favors a direct style of communication (tell it like it is), as opposed to indirect (find ways to agree and do not state the facts outright, especially if a disagreement could result). While I live and work in my culture, as an individual I tend to speak more indirectly than many around me. So while generalizations are helpful with a general understanding—of trends and tendencies—they do not apply to individuals. I can't say, "All Canadians are _____ (fill in the blank)" because Canada comprises thirty-five million individuals, all of whom are different from each other.

While it's helpful to understand Them better, eventually, either in this circumstance or another one, They will be different enough to upset you. You are still left with the difficulty of feeling upset when someone acts differently than you think they should—you still have the same urge to be right and make the Other wrong. This occurs when the differences between you become too pronounced to tolerate. This point is different for everyone—that point where you say, "That's going too far!"

So learning about other cultures, while interesting, is only of limited utility without an attempt to address the root cause of such conflicts.

Learning about other cultures' ways of life, values, and behaviors helps with empathy—it allows us to stretch our tolerance further than if we had no knowledge. An American manager sent to his company's office in Mexico would do better if he understood that Mexican workers generally value harmony, and that seeking to single out individuals or promote individual initiative at the expense of collective harmony might create significant discord in that location. If he did not have that knowledge, he would feel frustrated in trying to do business in the way he was accustomed to, and might even judge them negatively, because he can only see through his particular cultural view. If you learn that the guy at work who has been invalidating you for years is culturally taught to dismiss emotional expressiveness, you can understand better why he acts disdainfully toward you when you become animated in an argument.

Understanding allows more space for others to be who and what they are, but it does not and cannot go far enough. Even when you understand better, you will still become uncomfortable (annoyed, upset, angry) when you differ, if the difference is great enough or the issue matters enough to you.

Is cultural difference distinct from other types of difference? It's not. It is simply one aspect of difference between people. What is intolerance? It is attachment to our own beliefs; when we are attached to what we think we know, we judge the Other. Culture, and any kind of difference, is *fun*, interesting, and wonderful, and our differences inspire creativity. If the difference between people wasn't cultural, it would be something else. Do not take the nature of the difference seriously—do not take culture, or any set of ideas, seriously. Do not mistake culture or opinion for what someone is.

Universals?

And while there are many worlds, there are also Universals, which have the potential to bring us all together.

A young American, while visiting a Buddhist teacher in Tibet, asked him, "Have you ever read the Christian bible?"

"No—do read it to me," said the teacher. The student opened the Bible and read from Matthew:

"And why concern yourself with clothing? Consider the lilies of the field, how they grow. They toil not, neither do they spin, and yet I tell you that even Solomon in all his glory was not arrayed like one of these.... Take therefore no thought for the morrow, for the morrow will take thought for the things of itself."

The teacher said, "Whoever uttered those words I consider an enlightened man."

The student continued reading: "Ask and it shall be given you, seek and you will find, knock and it will be opened to you. For everyone that asks receives, and he that seeks finds, and to him that knocks, it shall be opened."

The teacher said, "That is excellent. Whoever said that is a Buddha."

Is it possible to see beyond our culture?

If we rely exclusively on the things our cultures teach us to make sense of the world, we find we are limited by them. They function as definers of who is in and who is out, what is acceptable and what is not. Liken culture to a map. If each of us has a map but they don't match, we can choose to fight over whose is correct, or we can carry them along with us and explore the world and our place in it—together. Perhaps we can recognize that each map is an individual fragment, valid but not universal—we can look to connecting with each other in a broader way. And this begins with a larger sense of self, which allows room for a larger framework outside of the constraints of culture. Can we hold both?

Culture, like the beings that compose it, constantly evolves. It is a means through which we share life experience, create, grow, connect, build, and solve problems. It is not, even as a source of differences between people, an impediment to be overcome, per se, but a wonderful means through which we can relate, connect, and grow. But to do so, we need to allow others to be as they are. When we do this, we release resistance and conserve energy. We don't fight what is, which opens the door for us to think about difference in a new way.

You Say Tomay-to, I Say Tomah-to...Let's Call the Whole Thing Off

EVERYONE RESPONDS TO DIFFERENCE IN HIS OR HER OWN UNIQUE WAY. SOME are very comfortable with a wide gulf between views, and others can tolerate very little divergence from their own ideas.

In the old movie *Auntie Mame*, a wealthy widow, adventurous and fascinated by life, wants to prevent her nephew from marrying a small-minded, snobbish woman. She arranges a dinner at her home, a meeting of the two "families" in advance of the wedding. She invites all of her eccentric friends—a yogi, a pregnant single mother—none of whom are "acceptable" in high society, and all of whom shock the highbrow family into canceling the wedding. They can't abide such unsavory company. This, of course, was her plan all along.

We all know people who love to be immersed in new and different things. They are open, curious, and ready to learn. Even so, we all experience at least some discomfort or unease when the gulf between our perspective and others' is large.

It's often uncomfortable when you notice the difference between yourself and another. You either feel the urge to make the other person see things your way, or you feel you have nothing in common—you are better than them, they are stupid, they are wrong, or they're "other" than you in some way. Not *like* you. This happens when we notice and focus on the things that are different, and not the things that are similar. When it's hard to find things about them that are similar to you.

We are mixing in very close quarters with others who are different in many ways. Our exposure to diversity has never been greater. When we perceive cultural differences in particular, they often impact us deeply, and we may have a strong emotional response to them. Culture is about how we live our lives, and there are many ways to live a life. It's simple when we think of our neighbors: we understand our lives differ, and it's OK. But, you see, you and your neighbors all share more or less the same cultural assumptions. They might all like different TV shows than you, have different lawnmowers, and your kids may go to different schools. We are comfortable, mostly, with that degree of difference. In many countries, people are even OK with the fact that others have different values and different religions.

But what about big differences, like divergent ideas about how women or children should be treated, or the importance of human rights? There comes a point for each of us when we become uncomfortable with difference—and this causes arguments and conflict at worst, dislike at best. We accept what a person is doing up to a point, after which it becomes "wrong." And our disagreements about the point at which it becomes wrong—or about what is right or wrong in living life—have been the source of all conflict on planet earth since we recorded time.

Socrates said: Know thyself. How do you respond to differences? Do you like experiencing a wide range of opinions, even on issues you feel strongly about? How do you act and feel when you don't care too much about the topic? How do you act and feel if the difference matters a lot to you? When we have a *positive* response to a difference, we will incorporate it, copy it, talk about it, imitate it, write about it, teach it, learn about it, adapt it, or embrace it. When we perceive a difference but don't care about it, we won't do anything with or about it. Nothing happens. When we have a *negative* response to a difference, we move away from it, argue against it, make rules about it, talk against it, write against it, teach against it, or fight it. What I think about any difference between us determines how I feel about it, and that shapes my response to you. That response in turn shapes all the events that flow from my choice.

It's natural to want to spend our time with people who are like us—in fact, similar things are always drawn together. But when Others do come across your experience, the question is, do you actively resist and avoid? Or actively embrace? If you can embrace, you understand the value of difference. As Stephen Covey said, "You think differently than me. I need to listen to you."

When something matters to us, it connects in some way to our values, which lie below the surface of our everyday awareness most of the time. Anytime something upsets you deeply, it has touched on your values—and your values spring from culture. Values are not visible, so we don't identify them easily in ourselves or others, and to complicate matters, we are rarely willing to talk about them either. Our anger is often a response to having our values challenged. We feel upset by a different opinion because our identities—given to us by our culture—

are connected to the values we have been taught. The values become wound up with our sense of self. We are so connected to the things we think (which flow from the values we absorb) and our beliefs (which are simply established patterns of the things we think) that when someone disagrees with us, we feel it's an attack on us *personally*, and not just an affront to our ideas or beliefs. It feels like it's *you* they are disagreeing with, instead of just your beliefs—this is how closely we hold our beliefs and values. In your own life, think about the most divisive thing, a constant source of conflict. Is it an opinion about something? There exists conflict because we *identify* with different ideas—this is what makes us feel upset, and makes us want to be right. Identifying—thinking that that idea, on some level, *is* us—is the problem. In fact, your beliefs are distinct from you. Like changing the software in your laptop computer, you can replace the beliefs you have with new ones...and still exist! Clearly, uprooting beliefs and replacing them is a much deeper and emotionally involved process than changing software. The point is that they are not synonymous with you.

Imagine driving along the highway with a friend. As the trip continues, your mind wanders until it fastens onto something you heard on the news that bothered you. You heard that there had been a recent rash of dog attacks in your city—each one involved a pit bull terrier attacking either another dog or a child, and in each case the injuries were serious. You always felt those dogs were dangerous, and now you think they should be banned altogether from your city. You turn to your friend and tell him what you think: "People shouldn't be allowed to own pit bulls—they are too dangerous!" Your friend, though, has a different opinion. He has friends who own such dogs, and in his experience, they are wonderful pets. He thinks your opinion is wrong, and tells you so. Now, this bugs you. When someone disagrees with your opinion, especially one you deeply believe and care about, it's annoying, isn't it? You *know* those dogs are bad news and are predisposed to aggression (substitute any other opinion here that you feel strongly about—politics, religion, the environment, etc.). But your friend *knows* that they are great dogs and just need responsible owners. You're annoyed now, and so you start proving your point: listing all the attacks you know of, and he does the same for the reverse argument. With each back-and-forth volley in the disagreement, you want more and more to be right, and are less and less willing to concede defeat. Each of you feels a growing irritation and desire to cling even more to your opinion as the right one. You are annoyed because you have identified with your opinion so closely that when someone attacks it, it feels like they are attacking *you*. That's why you feel upset. You *are*, in that situation, your opinion. If the argument grows any further, both people feel a deeper and deeper need to be right. Emotionally, it feels like if you are wrong, or if you surrender, it's almost like a death. If you did not identify with your opinion, you wouldn't care very much whether he agreed with you or not. Because we often unconsciously identify with, or think we are, our opinions and beliefs, these things are barriers to communicating and connecting with others.

We are, in fact, much more than our thoughts and values. If we are able to see that we exist apart from them, and that, because they are mental constructs, they are replaceable with different ones, then we see we are free to choose—whether to decide on a course of action independent of the mental constructs we have been taught, or not. Is there anything, after all, important enough to lose your peace of mind about?

Barriers: Through the Looking Glass

You are, right at this moment, a magnificent world. You are a compilation of many different thoughts, moods, characteristics, abilities, and experiences. You are body, mind, and spirit. Imagine yourself surrounded by many different layers of "being": one layer is your gender, one is your family, one is your education, your personal history, preferences, biases, socioeconomic status, physical makeup, emotions, thoughts, age and generation, birth order, job, marital status, etc. Each of these is an identity, a means to define ourselves—who we think we are, and who we are not. Each of these can function as something in common with certain people, and as something that separates us from other people. Each operates like a mini culture: my gender, eye color, height, age, number of children, etc. can make me the "same as" some people and "different than" others. My socioeconomic status makes me the "same as" those in my neighborhood with similar homes and cars and lifestyles, and "different than" those who do not share these things. These layers are like culture: they define who is "in" and who is "out." They function as connectors or as barriers. Gender will likely be a connecting factor when I am the only woman in a room full of men and notice another woman walking in. I will feel an affiliation with her on that basis alone, even if we are different in every other way.

You see the world through each of these layers, and identify with them. Each layer shapes how you see and understand the world around you. I see, think, and interpret within the context of all these aspects of "me."

When we communicate with others, all of whom are immersed in their own layers of being, we get interesting dynamics. We often imagine the process of communicating as linear—a straight line between two parties. We think a message can travel a straight path between the sender and the receiver. However, this is never the case. The message I send you will always be distorted, refracting like light through many invisible layers of identity I have inherited throughout my life—all those things I believe I am, and that compose my perspective on the world. The message between us must be filtered through my invisible layers, and then, to be received by you, filtered through your invisible layers. We perceive, speak, and listen through layers of filters. These layers, often things we are not even conscious of, serve as barriers that confuse and distort our messages.

Culture can be a barrier to understanding when we communicate with others. An obvious barrier is language; if we don't share the same language, that language difference is a barrier to communicating. Between cultures, other differences apply also: communication styles can differ in *how* you communicate, or *when* you communicate. Very emotionally expressive cultures have everyone speaking all at the same time and constantly interrupting (which shows interest and engagement in the conversation). This can be disconcerting for those accustomed to more restrained cultures in which one is expected to wait one's turn to speak. Each culture interprets the other's style as rude. That interpretation, stemming from culturally influenced behaviors, is a barrier.

Barriers to effective communication can confuse or distort the message and intention of the message being conveyed. This can result in failure of the communication process or another effect that is undesirable.

Essentially, a barrier is anything—a situation, style of talking, etc.—that gets in the way of effective communication.

When we see that the layers that surround us are not only barriers to communicating, but layers of *identity* too, then we can understand why conflict arises often in our lives. If I think, "I AM a _____" then we can easily affiliate with those who we think ARE that, too...but those who are NOT that are "outside." This categorization can either be a cause for interest, a barrier to communication, or, in the case of more deep differences, a catalyst for conflict. The history and hardships of a culture provide deep roots for the weaving together of common identity among its members, and often fertile fields for the growth of prejudice and intolerance regarding "outsiders," particularly those seen as responsible for those past hardships.

We inherit our sense of self from our culture. Our culture hands us a set of ideas (rules, expectations, assumptions—a whole worldview), which over time becomes an identity for us. We know through our culture who and what we are, what values we have, where we belong.

We take on these ideas, which include deeply held values, as our identity in the world. When we come across others who do not share our ideas, or who have different ideas, conflict often ensues because any disagreement with our ideas feels like a disagreement with *us*, personally. So we begin with a case of mistaken identity. Then it worsens: you disagree with me, so I defend myself or explain myself. In doing this I push back against you and your ideas. You push back to me, defending and explaining yourself. With each volley, the conflict becomes energized; each person experiences a growing need to be right, and the discomfort increases.

In a disagreement, we align ourselves along polarities—mine or yours, right or wrong, better or worse, more than or less than—and the polarity becomes more and more energized with every volley. The person you are arguing with (even in your mind) becomes the Other. The Other lives outside the set of ideas we have. The Other is irrational, misguided, or evil.

We take ourselves—and our ideas—seriously. In fact, we think we *are* our ideas a lot of the time!

ALLOWING

There was an old man who fell into a deep, swiftly flowing river, which swept him downstream before anyone could save him. The townspeople, fearing for his life, looked on. Miraculously, he came out alive and unharmed several miles downstream. They asked him how he managed to survive. "I accommodated the water, and did not curse it. Without thinking, I allowed myself to be shaped by it. By not fighting the momentum or direction of its flow, I allowed it to carry me. Plunging into the swirl, I came out with the swirl. This is how I survived."

Fighting the current in the river, or the fact he had fallen in, or the temperature of it, or even cursing the cause of his fall, are all fruitless uses of energy. Note that the man did not give up. He did not say, "Oh what's the point, I may as well drown." Yet, when we think about the idea of "surrender," this is often how we understand it. Instead, he retained his will to live, and worked *with* the situation. He flowed with the current, and "without thinking" (i.e. without resisting what is), he spent no time cursing or arguing. He let the river be as it is, he let the situation be as it is, he set aside the complaint he may have had against the cause of his fall, and he opened to the possibilities before him. Like the man allowing things to be as they were in the river story, we must allow each person to be as they are, also.

WHEN OTHERS DON'T MAKE SENSE

ONCE THERE WERE TWO MEN FISHING OFF A DOCK. A SCORPION HAPPENED by, and fell in the water. One man reached down and pulled it up out of the water. The scorpion stung him. He kept fishing, and a bit later, the scorpion fell in the water again. Again the man rescued it, and again he was stung. The other man said, "Why, when you know its nature is to sting, would you keep saving it?" "Because," the first man replied, "it's my nature to save it."

Many people would say that the man who subjected himself to that kind of danger was crazy—that he shouldn't expose himself like that.

If he were a father, perhaps we'd say he was irresponsible. Yet there is no denying what his wish was: to do what his heart or conscience bid him to do.

Years ago I read a story about a woman who sought advice at a local hospital regarding a mass on her lower jaw.[6] It was swiftly identified as cancerous, and a highly trained medical team went to work determining the type of cancer, severity, and treatment she would need. It was clear that without both chemotherapy and removal of the mass (including her lower jaw) she would die. They met with her and her family, explained everything, and got ready to book the surgery. They were incredulous when she and her family refused the proposed treatments. So, the team assumed they had not been clear enough. They explained that without the treatment they suggested, she would die very soon. They showed her and her family the statistics on survival rates, and explained she could live a full lifespan if she went ahead with their recommendations. They all graciously thanked the team, again refused the assistance, and prepared to leave. Observers of that encounter noted that the woman was calm and dignified throughout, as was her loving family. She signed a release form indicating she had received medical advice. The staff involved in the case was shaken—they felt frustrated and judgmental about her decision. Why did she refuse? Nobody knew. They just couldn't understand what would make a person do that. We will never know what was in her heart and mind, or her family's. But even if we did, some of us would still judge her decision, while others might support it. Regardless of whether her reasoning was supportable or not—and we might ask who would be the judge of that in any event—she made the decision. We can allow it, or not. Have you ever tried to convince a friend to do something, and they were determined not to? I had the perfect job lined up for my friend Aimee years ago. She'd been struggling with finances for

---

6   Remen, Rachel Naomi, M.D., *Kitchen Table Wisdom: Stories That Heal* (New York: Riverhead Books. 1996) p. 200

ages, she was full of talent, and I just knew this job was perfect for her. But when I proudly presented the opportunity to her, she flatly, though politely, refused. I was stunned. This would solve all her problems, wouldn't it? It would provide a good income and security, was a short commute, and paid really well. I cajoled, I wheedled, I begged her to take it. After all, I was worried about her. But she proudly told me she wanted to create her own company on her own terms, be her own boss, and create her own paycheck. My opinions fell on deaf ears. I passionately wanted a certain result, but was met with a "brick wall" in this situation. I could accept it, or not. Accepting it meant letting her be who she was and go her own way, no matter how much I wanted her to do otherwise. Allowing meant *freely* accepting, so that my inner space remained free of contaminants like resentment or irritation. Allowing, simply, meant dropping the matter altogether. Not doing so would mean keeping the disagreement alive, and expecting her to yield to my opinion (using guilt, perhaps, or sheer force of will).

We must allow people to be as they are. It's futile to complain about or push against situations or people, wishing they were different than they are. We need not aim to correct them or argue with them. We don't need to "set them straight." It is better to accept and work with the materials we have, and understand that doing otherwise is a waste of energy. We need to accept what is. Sometimes, accepting and allowing means dropping our end of the conflict, and sometimes it means dropping the barriers we have that separate us from others. How do we do that? By being in the present moment, listening to each other, understanding the power of the stories we tell ourselves, thinking critically about those stories, and cultivating a true appreciation of difference. Allowing and accepting clears our minds, builds goodwill, builds bridges, and conserves energy.

The deepest and best respect you can give someone is acceptance. Allowing is freely accepting them as they are, without condition. When we accept and allow, we stop trying to control things, situations, and people that ultimately we cannot control. It is letting them be, and letting go of the expectation that they should be different than they really are. If you reflected honestly on the instances you wanted someone to change something to suit you (their opinion or behavior, for example) you'd notice that it was an effort to make yourself feel better. It's an open question as to whether anyone can credibly demand this from another or not. Personally, I believe we should each be responsible for our own contentment, and leave others out of it. Allowing and accepting are synonymous with true respect. Have you known anyone who accepted you just the way you are, and never required you to change?

For example, everybody is a walking contradiction in some ways. I know perfectly balanced, rational people who occasionally insist on having opinions that fly in the face of common sense. I'll bet you do, too. Don't be upset when they aren't making sense, aren't being "reasonable," aren't being agreeable, or aren't doing what they should be doing. You may be right, but instead of trying to straighten them all out, just relax and let them think what they want to think, and be as they wish to be. Rare is the person who, when presented with a different opinion, or with evidence showing they are incorrect, says, "Well isn't that interesting. Now I know that, my opinion has changed!" Instead, I have observed that we prefer to stick to our same opinions like barnacles on a sinking ship, no matter what. No amount of shaking, convincing, or cajoling can pry us loose. And so, after we have spoken our piece, should we have chosen to, the best course is often to let the Other be, content in their certitude.

There is a story of a beautiful village girl who had gotten pregnant. Her parents were furious, and demanded to know who the father was. Desperate, the anxious girl finally pointed to the village wise man, who was revered by everyone for living a pure life. When the outraged parents confronted the wise man with their daughter's accusation, he simply replied, "Is that so?" When the baby was born, the parents brought it to the wise man, who now was despised by the whole village. They demanded that he take care of the child, since it was his responsibility. "Is that so?" he said calmly as he accepted the baby. For many months he took good care of the child until the daughter could no longer withstand the lie she had told. She confessed the baby's real father was a young man in the village whom she had tried to protect. The parents immediately went to the wise man to ask that he return the baby. Apologizing profusely, they explained what had happened. "Is that so?" the wise man said as he handed them the child.

Difference—diversity—simply is. It exists, and is a fact of life. We are all surrounded by diverse people, ideas, judgements, standards, opinions, responses, attitudes, and ways of getting through the day. If we can relax into this reality, we can stop pushing against all the things in this world that bother us, and use our energies to create outcomes that we prefer. As we will see, attempting to control others, or any external factors, in an effort to make what we dislike go away, requires more energy that it is worth, and in the long run is an unsuccessful strategy.

> *"Give yourself permission to allow this moment to be exactly as it is, and allow yourself to be exactly as you are."*
>
> —*Jon Kabat-Zinn*

Allowing (some call it surrendering) is not a passive approach. There is great power and purpose in it: we do not fight what already exists, in order that we conserve our energy and direct it in a way we choose—toward things we *can* do something about.

A nurse told me a moving story about a man in her care years ago who had terminal cancer. He related that before his cancer arrived, he was focused on possessing things, or, as he put it, "stuff." Happiness, for him, was dependent on "having stuff." When he had the job, the girlfriend, the promotion, the success, the money, he was happy. When he didn't, he was depressed. Lying in bed recovering from a cancer treatment, he reflected that he spent his life up to that point trying to hang on to his possessions, afraid they would be taken away or he'd lose them somehow. He noticed the similarity with his two-year-old niece: she was happy when she had candy, but cried when it fell on the floor or it was taken away. His happiness depended on having his possessions. He spent his time worrying about what would happen to them and guarding against losing them, and in the process, never actually derived real pleasure from them. He survived the cancer, and the time it gave him to reflect on life changed him forever. For the first time he is truly happy, independent of the weather, of the economy, of everything, because he chooses it every day. He learned his happiness had nothing to do with outside factors, and everything to do with personal choice. Now he doesn't need anything to be different in order to be happy. He allows things to be as they are, and has, in so doing, set himself free.

Can you let people be who and what they are?

We need to look at the process and dynamics of "against-ness," *not the actual content*. The content changes with the weather, and so is not relevant. Like scenery, it changes, and so it is a distraction.

Does allowing others to be as they are mean we are passively accepting our fate? Does it mean being a doormat for others' ill will? Allowing means not resisting what is. To fight what already is by saying it shouldn't be so, is a little insane. We can observe a situation without insisting it be other than it is, and from that place of acceptance make a decision—either to try to change it, to leave the situation, or to let it be as it is. With respect to other people, there is nothing wrong with putting forward your thoughts, or stating your truth, clearly and simply. Others may hear it or not, may heed it or not—but allowing them to react as they will is important. The moment you begin arguing is the moment you stop allowing. Let them have a different idea, let them be wrong-headed, let them disagree. You cannot change them, and rarely can you get them to change their opinion and agree with yours instead. Let them be "right," and see for yourself the sense of freedom and clarity you achieve as a result.

As Within, So Without: A Shift in Perspective

YOUR INNER PEACE CREATES PEACE IN THE WORLD.

You cannot create peace around you unless you have it within you. This sounds like common sense, but observe: how much anger is often present in those trying to enforce peace? It's often an angry parent yelling at the kids to "stop fighting!" It's an angry teacher yelling, "just get along!" If your inner world is upset, you will behave accordingly, and it will be reflected in the circumstances around you. Imagine waves spreading out from you with each thought, word, and action. You are an agent in the world, and all you think, say, and do sends waves outward that affect, like ripples in a pond, all the world around you. Moreover, everything that comes to you is a reflection of what you send out. What you put out is what you get back. If you plant an apple seed, you will get an apple tree. You will not get an orange tree. Even if you stomp around and demand an orange tree, you won't get it because you haven't planted it. Gentle waves of peace cannot emanate from an angry heart any more than tiny ripples can emanate from a boulder thrown in a pond. The nature and frequency of each does not match.

We habitually look outside ourselves for answers. We are not accustomed to looking within first for an understanding of the circumstances in which we find ourselves. When we feel bad in a relationship, we want the other person to do things differently so we can feel better, or more comfortable. We want to find the cause "out there," and force it to be different than it is so we can feel better. But this task is futile and never-ending. To get peace, we must be peace. To receive happiness, we must be happy. We are actually the point of origin of any state we wish to experience! The world presents us with a never-ending array of people, places, and things that we try to change, to make them conform to what we think is best. We want the wars out there to stop. We want unkindness to stop. But the change in the world we wish for must match what we have within ourselves and what we are sending out, or it cannot be. The focus remains within us at all times. Let's not try to change "Them." Let's look within and see how we can change the signals we are sending out.

"What others do and do not do is not my concern," said the Buddha. "What I do and do not do—that is my concern."

War begins in each human heart...and can only end there. If war did not live within the breast of humans, there would be no wars in evidence outside us. Conflict in the world is simply a larger scale of the conflict we find in our own lives.

I know a woman who is embroiled in constant struggle with her ex-husband. He sends her emails accusing her of all kinds of things, and she finds herself constantly on the defensive. I asked her what would happen if she just let go of her resistance and let him feel he is right. Any attempt to correct him or defend herself, of course, results in a worsening of the situation. "But it's not fair!" she insists. "He thinks I am a poor parent, and should be doing this, and not doing that...he's so wrong! He needs to know that. He shouldn't be allowed to get away with that." He is not, however, interested in the truth as she sees it, or in her perspective. And if she can accept the fact of it, she can drop her expectation that he should be reasonable (i.e. different than he is). It is as it is. She can state the truth, simply and with power, and then choose not to energize the conflict further by entertaining his contradictions. To do this, she needs to release her negativity and judgement about what is happening, because that is the fuel for the resistance, and thus fuel for the conflict.

A wise mentor once said to me, "Do you want to be happy or do you want to be right?" Right now, my friend has deeply negative feelings and reactions to her ex's accusations. While understandable, her inner dynamic must change in order for her to see and experience something different on the outside. My friend can speak her truth, and still remain nonresistant in the relationship, not reacting on the basis of negativity in response to an external irritant like her ex's accusations, but on the basis of an inner alignment with the situation as it is. She would be flowing with what is happening, not against it. From this stance comes an ability to think and act with true power and clarity—it is only from this nonresistant place that change can come about This is a profound, though subtle, shift in approach that makes an enormous difference in any conflict situation.

There is a difference, in other words, between a resistant *No* (you don't like what is happening and don't want it to be there) and a nonresistant *No* (stating something almost as a matter of fact or observation). The former is negative, the latter is not.

Being nonresistant in this situation does not necessarily mean she would let herself be abused or manipulated. She can say, "No" or "That is false" or state what is true of the situation from her perspective while at the same time not entertaining negativity. She can say the *No* clearly and from an inner place of integrity without "pushing against" any particular wrongdoing. You can recognize a situation as it is without judging it, and thereby resisting it.

When she reacts according to her negativity and judgements about her ex or what he is doing, she energizes the conflict. *As within, so without—negativity (resistance) within yourself yields negativity in external circumstances.* Imagine asserting an argument or defending yourself verbally—in either case you are pushing against something (the other person's ideas, for example). When you are both pushing, each assertion becomes like a wall of energy. The dispute becomes energized and grows. When there is no resistance, though, the quality of the interaction is profoundly changed. Imagine pushing against a wall – the wall is just like the palpable energy field of anger (resistance) that surrounds you each of you when in an argument. Now imagine the wall suddenly disappearing. There is nothing to push up against. One person has changed the dynamic simply by not resisting .

Our focus can move from changing and controlling the outer world (structures, rules, people) to reshaping our inner world, consciously and voluntarily, in the collective desire for peace. This is the only place we can begin, the only thing we can do anything about as individuals. It is important to begin on the personal, inner level—all meaningful change needs to begin there.

A friend was very concerned about her brother making poor decisions and ruining his life. He was going out with a girl who apparently was a destructive influence. My friend was anxious to "straighten him out" by helping him see the error of his ways. She wanted to set him on a healthier path. He could do so much better with his life! Her concern was so great she was obsessing about his well-being, even losing sleep some nights because he was not heeding her advice. She shared this with me over lunch one day. I vaguely waved my hand and spoke generally about how others need to walk their own path, and we need to let them, no matter how uncomfortable this might be. This struck her as far too laissez-faire; someone's welfare was at stake! I remained vague and positive—to the frustration of my friend, who never again consulted me when someone needed "straightening out."

And to take on the job of determining the right thing to do in another's life feels a bit...exhausting. I wouldn't know where to begin with the details needed to manage such a task. When you allow others to be as they are, there is great relief. Now you don't have to worry about what they are doing wrong, or what they should do better, or how you can make them see the error of their ways. The relief washes right over you. Let it be. Let them be. Respect them enough to let them determine their own way.

Allowing is respect. After all, can anyone really know enough about you and your journey in life to set *you* straight?

There are people in your life who think impossible things, things that to you are clearly wrong. They have beliefs that are far outside of what you see before your eyes. What then? There is only one thing. Allow them to be and think as they are. You can speak the truth as you see it and not demand that it be adopted by anyone else.

Each person, no matter their form or substance, is a necessary part of the whole. Attempting to pull one thread, to remove it because it does not appear to fit (attitude, morals, behavior, appearance, or culture) is to compromise the tapestry. Each part of creation is inseparable from all the rest, despite appearances. And while we may not understand the benefit that one person's role may play in the overall tapestry of creation, we can stop resisting its existence and work with what we can.

What Is, Is

There is conflict, there is suffering, there is war. Whether we like it or not, these things are—they exist. Our opinions and judgements about whether they *should* exist have no effect at all on the situation. When you travel to a foreign country whose culture is different than yours, you often need to modify your dress and behavior if you are to be safe, particularly if you are female. *Should* you be able to wear what you want, and go wherever you want in the new country? Your answer will depend on your culture, to a great extent. But your opinion about what "should" be is, for practical purposes, irrelevant. It makes practical sense to recognize what is: different cultural norms and expectations for women in the new country. Adapting to them respects the new culture and you as well. Are you going to have much success resisting what is? You could lecture them all, or perhaps demand that they change their history and traditions to suit your ideas of what is appropriate. These are forms of judgement, another way we "push against." You could also do as you please and take your chances.

There will always be duality—things we like and things we don't, opposites, differences, and contrasting circumstances. Duality exists in all things. *It is never the thing itself that poses a problem for us; it is our thoughts, or judgements, about it.* When it is raining outside, I might like the rain or not, but disliking it does nothing other than make me upset. The rain, I believe, is indifferent to whether I like it or not. My attitude about it doesn't, by itself, change its existence. If I can recognize it is raining (which is an inherently neutral situation) and make appropriate preparations, I have accepted what is. All things are neutral, no matter how they appear. It is our definitions and attitudes about them that create what they mean to us.

Strangely, human beings spend a great deal of time and energy arguing with what is. We notice what's "wrong" and lament it, complain about it, hate it, petition against it, feel upset by it, worry about it, dig deeper into it. Since pushing against "what is" is futile, we can allow ourselves now to relax, at least long enough to let what is be. We need to allow, lighten up, let others be, relax. We need to let everyone and everything be as they are, as it is.

The world is on the move; millions of people are moving between countries and cultures—more than ever before in history. There are more people than ever before more connected by a global economy than ever before. We are connecting with more ideas, more possibilities, more people, and more perspectives than ever before. As the famous Borg said in *Star Trek: The Next Generation*, "Resistance is futile; you will be assimilated." The future is here, now. We need to be friends with this. It is more efficient and effective than resisting it or trying to control everybody. Change and the discomfort that accompanies it is an eternal fact of life. If we can manage to become friends with the diverse climate we find ourselves in, and make friends with the idea of allowing everyone to be as they are, we'll have much more fun along the way, and experience the freedom of not needing things to be a certain way in order to feel better.

When you allow things and people to be as they are, you are not resisting. And when you are not resisting, you are not opposing or judging. Others do not meet you with resistance in return, and you find it easier to build connections and understanding with others.

Next we'll talk about how to accept and allow, through listening, critical thinking and being present in the moment. The immediate benefits you will experience using these ideas is decreased friction in all areas of your life, release of the tension that accompanies it, and a true and lasting inner peace.

How to Accept and Allow:

a) Stories

The Power of Story

Stories have enormous power to inspire, incite, discourage, or empower. Stories of legendary heroes and villains have changed the world: David and Goliath, Beauty and the Beast, Cinderella, The Hare and the Tortoise, The Hobbit, The Lord of the Rings, the Velveteen Rabbit, etc. We love and retell these stories because they entertain and amuse. Yet on a deeper level we resonate with the messages they bear for us: "Believe in your dreams and they will come true," "True love sees beyond form," "Slow and steady wins in the end," "Good is stronger than evil," etc.

The storytellers bring to life images, emotions, and desires with their artfully woven words. While the authors of these well-known tales are seen as "real" storytellers, the truth is, we are all storytellers. We tell our stories all day long, all our lives long—to ourselves and others. What's more, we actually "live into" our stories, so how we tell them is incredibly important. Our thoughts weave our stories and create our lives.

We look for meaning in our lives. We want people and events to fit together and make sense to us. Our brains are designed to do this. In our minds, we weave the pieces of our lives into place—into a story—effortlessly. We assign ourselves roles, write other characters into the plot, and create the story with our thoughts, emotions, and actions. We are brilliant at it—so good that it's effortless, so effortless we often do not realize we are doing it. We do it unconsciously much of the time.

We all tell stories. When you are asked in a job interview to "tell us a bit about yourself," you are creating a story, or relating a story you created long ago. Stories allow us to make sense out of our lives. They help us create meaning out of the events we experience, and they shape our lives and how we live them. We interpret everything around us—and we do so uniquely. We are not neutral recorders and storers of factual data, though we might like to think so. I see an event a particular way—through the filters of my culture, background, education, gender, biases, life experiences—and I weave together, in thought, the bits that I perceived through my senses. Where there are information gaps, my mind fills in the story seamlessly with ideas that have been stored in my mind from the past. We do not *extract* meaning from our environment—we *make* it. *We* are the meaning makers in our lives, the storytellers. Our stories, if we repeat them often enough, become real to us and we begin to see our world in terms of the stories we have told. When we encounter information that does not fit the story we have woven, we often will not "notice" it. Details that don't fit the stories we believe get left by the wayside.

> *"The world will persist in exhibiting before you what you persist in affirming the world is."*
>
> —*Emma Curtis Hopkins*

These stories feel real, and almost everything we live through each moment of each day reinforces them. Emotion lends power to our stories: when we have a thought, our bodies respond with different chemical responses depending on the emotion that arises from the thought. Thoughts that are repeated often, and have strong emotions attached to them, create very "deep" pathways in our brains. They become familiar, so that when similar events crop up in your life, the brain recognizes it and triggers the same landslide of chemical reactions; your responses become automatic for all things that trigger the brain's recognition. And you act—inwardly in the form of inner dialogue and outwardly in the form of choices and behaviors—in accordance with those automatic responses. This is how we come to "live our stories": we have familiar thoughts about ourselves, nestled inside a familiar belief context about ourselves. We think, feel, and act consistently with them.

So if a person's story is:

"Life is hard. I have always had to struggle, and nothing ever comes easily to me. I work twice as hard as most people I know, and never get paid enough for the time I put in. There is never enough time in the day, and I am constantly having to race to keep up. My efforts are never appreciated. I will always have to work like this; I cannot see any way out. It's not like I can retire early; I don't have enough money and I doubt I ever will."

This story comes along with feelings of anger, resentment, and fear. In the body, one might feel an adrenalin-like sensation in the solar plexus or chest.

This story's main character is portrayed as an underpaid, over-worked, unappreciated victim of unfair circumstances. That is the central theme in all interactions that person has all day long: it shapes her perception of the people around her, and all the events in her day. Thus, it shapes the choices she will make, and how she reacts to others. Once she acts in accordance with her perception, she has reinforced the story and it becomes "real": others react to her in accordance with her expectations (her attitude, body language, manner of speaking, and posture show what she is expecting), and all her choices create the ongoing, self-reinforcing loop that looks true. It's all she can see. She looks out at others and the world and says to herself, "See? They don't appreciate me, and I am overworked, and underpaid, and nothing ever works out for me." She has created her own story based on a belief system that reinforces itself, so it looks "true."

"Everything we hear is an opinion, not a fact. Everything we see is a perspective, not the truth."

- Marcus Aurelius

People's stories are part of their sense of self—in it, they are the star player, and they have reasons for casting themselves and others into the roles they do. Do not expect them to tell a different story, or to separate themselves from the stories they tell. But do try to loosen your hold on your own stories.

Do you know your own stories? Think of a life event. Are you the hero? The victor or the vanquished? The villain or victim? Do you tell a story of hardship or personal power? Do you talk about how life or your past has done you wrong?

The great news is that our stories are completely in our control. This knowledge is one of the most powerful tools we have in life. We are the authors of our own stories: we decide what the protagonist is like—what she thinks, feels, and does. We determine her style, how she speaks to people, her personal environment, her work style, how she walks, how she thinks, her disposition (cheerful, powerful, etc.). We determine the meaning of the events in her life, and how she responds to them. We can thus affect the plot of the story to a great extent. What we might regard as "fate," such as a life-changing event, can have a completely different meaning depending on who is defining it and what their perspective is. There is no meaning "out there." It is bestowed by the observer, the story maker.

Understanding the nature of stories and that they are woven out of beliefs that are not objective "truths" helps us detach from our own stories and understand others' attachment to theirs at the same time. People's stories are a part of them, and as such, we need to respect them. We must be critically aware of the stories we tell ourselves (about others) and respectful of the stories that others believe and tell themselves, too. In doing this, we loosen our attachment—our un-questioning allegiance—to our own stories. This is one way we can help us allow others to be just as they are.

A colleague I knew years ago was involved in a car crash that left her with some permanent facial scarring and limited mobility in one leg. She emerged from the trauma well enough, but over time became more and more focused on the injustice of the whole situation. Be-cause of "that idiot" (the driver of the other car) she suffered pain, in-convenience, and unhappiness. Within a year after the accident, "that idiot" was the cause of her depression, drug addiction, failed marriage, and a litany of other wrongs that had befallen her. As this general mal-aise developed, she was unable to hear others' perspectives on her sit-uation. Well-meaning people in her office had coordinated an effort to make her return to work more comfortable by arranging her workspace and schedule to accommodate her limitations. But to her, working was "impossible," a downslide "inevitable." Her story did not allow for the possibility of better endings; her thoughts, increasingly embittered, closed off anything resembling a solution. She argued with anyone who tried to offer her one. This woman's story about being a victim of "that idiot" was very important to her, and became an identity for her. Soon, she could see herself in no other way. Beliefs are not small things and are very key in people's sense of who they are.

Beliefs are really thoughts that have been repeated over and over again. They gain momentum over time. Remember what is actual-ly happening when you are upset because of a difference of opinion: you are upset because criticism of your opinion feels like an attack on *you*. You identify so closely with your ideas and opinions that you, in a sense, *are* them. The same identification takes place with beliefs— only more so. As you think and believe, so shall it be. If you believe you are a victim in any circumstance, you will identify with that story. You will defend your belief that it is true. People and events around you will prove to you that it's true. You will be hostile to anyone who suggests otherwise. You *are* that. Only when you can put some distance between yourself and the belief is another ending to the story possible.

Destiny

During a momentous battle, an army general decided to attack the enemy's position even though his army was dramatically outnumbered. He was confident they would win, but his men were filled with doubt. On the way to war, they stopped at a religious shrine. After praying with the men, the general took out a coin and said, "I shall now toss this coin. If it is heads, we shall win. If tails, we shall lose. Destiny will now reveal itself." He threw the coin into the air and everyone watched intently as it landed. It was heads. The soldiers were so overjoyed and filled with confidence that they vigorously attacked the enemy and were victorious.

After the battle, a lieutenant remarked to the general, "No one can change destiny."

"Quite right," the general replied as he showed the lieutenant the coin, which had heads on both sides.

The Possibility in Critical Thinking

Diversity facilitators sometimes ask, at the beginning of a workshop, that participants try to be at least minimally self-critical about their beliefs and personal identity. This is hard for us to do, because the world we experience shapes itself according to our beliefs and stories! Things are "true" to us because we believe they are. They are not "true" to begin with. Belief is the primary cause. We need to question our thoughts—about what we believe, about what others tell us, about what we think is true. A lot of the time we are not consciously aware of what we think and believe. When we become aware of our thinking—and to do this we need to be willing to notice and question what it is we are thinking—then we see the world differently.

Let's practice questioning our thoughts. Here's a thought: there shouldn't be violence in the world. It's wrong, it hurts people, children suffer, and you feel terrible when you think of it. You feel terrible because of the thought, not the violence in the world. The violence is. Our thoughts about it create all kinds of problems through our pushing against it. You might think there shouldn't be violence in the world. But your "shoulds" and "shouldn'ts" have no bearing on it at all. Whether you think there should be violence or not, it does exist. When we stop arguing with what is—in this case, the existence of violence in the world—we are in a much better position to do something about the situation. We can direct our efforts toward what we can do about it. Why do we need to think critically about our thoughts and beliefs? Some of our thoughts and beliefs serve us and are helpful, but many more are not. We seldom realize we are at liberty to choose our thoughts and beliefs, and to replace ones which do not serve us with ones that do.

Critical thinking demands that we allow for and conceive of alternate possibilities, and therefore expands our perspective. On a cloudy day, it looks like the world is gray. But if you go up in an airplane on that same day, you see that it's really sunny: the sky is blue. You could not see that it was a layer of clouds that made the world appear gray when you were on the ground. But if you kept going higher, outside the biosphere, you would see that the sky is actually black. Below that, you could not see that it is the biosphere that makes the sky appear blue. From space, then, you have an even more expanded perspective, which includes the understanding ("truth") that the sky is gray (under the clouds), and blue (above the clouds), and black (outside the biosphere)—all at the same time. They are all true, and represent different levels of perception and awareness. In space you see the sun is actually a star, then you see it is one star among many, and on into larger and larger frames of "reality." When things appear to us to be a certain way, you can be sure that they will look very different from a different perspective on the same event. All perspectives are true. And even though they look different, they can all coexist.

> *"Believe nothing, no matter where you read it, or who said it, no matter if I have said it, unless it agrees with your own reason and your own common sense."*
>
> —*The Buddha*

The Power of Belief

Your thoughts create your life. Your thoughts, repeated over and over, become your beliefs. Beliefs are powerful and self-reinforcing. If I believe life is a struggle, that is exactly what my life will be—until I change my idea about it. Imagine two people sitting next to each other on a bus: one mentally living in heaven and the other in hell. Even though they occupy the same moment in time and the same vehicle, they share none of the same thoughts. Each goes home to a completely different world, sewn together by their repeated thoughts. Looking at them seated side-by-side on the bus, it looks like they share the same reality.

A neighbor I know had very strong views of the world and the people in it. But then I'd spend time with those same people and realize they were nothing like he said. I did not see with the same "eyes"—I had a completely different perception and experience of them than he did.

His beliefs about people structured his expectations about them, and thus his own actions and words toward them. He believed they were nasty, and so dealt with them and thought about them in a hostile and fearful manner. All the while he wove more material into his inner story about their nastiness, and this in turn perpetuated the "reality" of his beliefs. After a while, we believe things because we think they are true. Really, it's nothing of the sort; we believe things, and *because* we believe them, they are "true"—for us. Science tells us that we do not experience "reality" directly. Our perceptions of it are filtered by our physical senses, plus our beliefs (created by culture, genetics, personal habits, etc.). We don't, for example, perceive the color in objects around us directly with our eyes. It does not exist "out there." Instead, our brains add color in through an interpretive process. Our brains see what they expect to see, and, similarly, we are in the habit of weaving stories around gaps in information to be able to conclude things (to feel like we know). Our bodies and minds cocreate reality—it is not an objective thing "out there." So if we cultivate an accepting way of being, plus an open and positive attitude, the outer world can correspond to our perception of it. It always does: if we are pessimists, we know the world will reflect this attitude back—and events will continue to support that idea. But there is nothing to suggest this is a fixed condition!

Judging Others' Beliefs

Before we judge what others believe, we'd best be aware of and take a close look at all the things we believe ourselves. Many things we believe either consciously or way down inside are downright odd. So what makes one different, or better, than the other? I know beautiful women who believe they are not pretty enough. I always want to ask, "For what?" Many older people were raised with the idea that children should be seen and not heard. I have met perfectly rational people who believe that the Day of Judgement—or the apocalypse—is at hand. In fact, there are many who are right now engaged with full belief in the idea that they are in an apocalyptic struggle. I knew a handsome, intelligent lawyer who truly believed that if a woman talked back to her spouse, her spouse had the right to punish her (including by hitting). I meet people every day who believe they are victims of fate, and others who believe that they are deeply unworthy no matter what they do in life. I myself have harbored a number of odd beliefs about myself and other people.

People believe things that defy what we think are facts. Are they entitled to believe as they do? Absolutely. Can I do anything about what they believe? I have some options: I can scorn them (in hopes that they see the error of their ways and come to some "sense"—mine, that is); I can argue (and try to force them to see "reason"—again, mine); or I can cajole them (by persuading them to think different things). None of these approaches, as you know in your own experience, works. As we have discussed, people believe and think what they want and what works for them; only their own experience combined with voluntary rethinking will change their minds. Everyone is free to do this—or not.

But why would I undertake to correct them? To be right, of course. I need to ask: "Why does it matter that I am right?" We can all ask ourselves this.

Let's rethink what we view to be facts, as well. The point is: let's not worry too much about what everybody else believes. Let's hold their ideas lightly—and better yet, let's hold our own ideas lightly too. What I think is correct today could easily be wrong tomorrow, and same for you. We can dance together without needing to be right, can't we?

Our minds, in their desire to know and thus help us feel more in control of our surroundings, mistake opinions for the truth. But how you interpret your life or someone else's, how you judge a situation, is no more than a viewpoint, and one of many possible perspectives.

"There is no right or wrong but thinking makes it so."

—*Shakespeare*

Shakespeare means here that there is no objective right or wrong. This means we decide the meaning of things for ourselves. Truth and everything else, then, is relative and not absolute. There is no inbuilt meaning in anything. We are the meaning makers, the story makers in our lives. If somebody crashes into my vehicle this morning, I can write my own story about that.

This event means: things are out of control in my life, or bad things keep happening to me, or this is a wakeup call in my life, or this is a gift to remind me to pay more attention in the present moment, or they are out to get me, or this is a way to finally get myself a new car after the insurance settlement, or those immigrants are terrible drivers, etc. (Pick the meaning you prefer.)

Once, a man pulled into a gas station on a country road and asked the gas station attendant, "What are the people like in the next town up ahead?" The attendant said, "What were the people like in the town you just came from?" "They were awful people!" the man responded. "I thought they were rude, cold, hostile, and unfriendly. They wouldn't give me the time of day." "Well," said the attendant, "I'm sorry to say it, but you're going to find exactly the same sort of people in the next town up ahead." Upset, the man drove off.

A bit later, another driver pulled in, heading in the same direction as the first. "What are the people like in the next town up ahead?" the second man asked. The attendant said, "What were the people like in the town you just came from?" "They were wonderful people," the second man responded. "I found them to be friendly, helpful, patient, and kind. They always went out of their way to help a stranger." "Well," said the attendant, "I'm happy to tell you that you're going to find exactly the same kind of people in the next town up ahead."

Once upon a time in India, Lord Krishna wished to see if the kings of his land were wise. First he called a feared and hated ruler named Duryodana. Lord Krishna told Duryodana that he was to take a journey throughout the lands. "I want you," Lord Krishna said, "to find one truly good person for me."

Duryodana obeyed Lord Krishna and began his travels. He found many different kinds of people and spoke to them about many things. After a long time away, Duryodana returned to Lord Krishna and said, "Lord, I have done what you commanded me and looked the whole world over for one truly good soul. Such a person I could not find. Each one I met was selfish and evil-minded. A truly good person cannot be found anywhere!"

Lord Krishna sent Duryodana on his way and called King Dhammaraja to see him. Dhammaraja was known as a kind man who tried to help people in his kingdom, all of whom loved him very much. Lord Krishna said to King Dhammaraja, "I want you to journey throughout all the lands and find me one truly evil person." Dhammaraja said, "As you wish, my Lord," and like Duryodana, he set off on a long journey.

After much time had passed, Dhammaraja came to Lord Krishna and said, "My Lord, I have not brought back the one truly evil person you wished to see. I found that people make mistakes; I found that they are fooled by others; I found that they act as if they are blind. But I could not find a truly evil person. The people are all good in their hearts!"[7]

We are meaning makers, and we use stories, which are woven from beliefs, to do this. We have the power to define *what* is positive and negative, since things do not in and of themselves have any meaning.

---

7 Zerah, Aaron, *How the Children Became Stars: A Family Treasury of Stories, Prayers and Blessings from Around the World.* (Notre Dame, Indiana: Sorin Books. 2000)

If an event *is*, who is the authority in determining if it's positive or negative? We can only say from this or that perspective if it could be positive or negative—but the perceiver is the one who ultimately assigns meaning to an event. Why not be a bit more playful with our interpretations and definitions? Does your perpetually small bank account really mean that you are unsuccessful? Does the fact that others dislike your art really mean you are a bad artist? You are free to define either situation in a way you prefer. Perhaps others dislike your art because it's ahead of its time! Personally, I have freed myself from many crippling beliefs which, exposed to the light of day, look absurd. But many beliefs we have were put into us as children, when we had no capacity to question them, and there they stay until we notice and—especially—question them. As I have learned, though they look real, they are simply monsters in the closet whose shadows we fear. We can replace them with new ones quite simply if we want to.

We can detach from our stories; my Granny always said, "This too shall pass." She often said that when I was complaining about an upcoming exam, or challenges I was facing, though I have concluded it applies to things going well, also. Hearing the phrase gave me a feeling of relief, and I think it's because it helped me to detach—to put distance between a situation and my story about it. Detachment lets us take a bigger view: things do change, so there is nothing to worry about in an absolute sense. As Byron Katie says, we don't suffer because of what happens, we suffer because of our thoughts, or stories, *about* what happens. Reality, like the soil, is neither good nor bad; it is inherently neutral. Only our thoughts make a thing "good" or "bad." In fact, it is *only* our thoughts that make us unhappy. It is never the event or person itself that makes us unhappy, but our thoughts about them, or our thoughts about what the situation "obviously" means. Human beings are meaning makers. There is nothing real about the meaning of the situation or a person's behavior, per se.

When we are wound up in our stories we cannot see out—our stories become our reality. Our thoughts create our lives. But if you question your thinking and the stories you tell yourself—about other people, about the world—then you give yourself the clarity you need to do something about a problem, if you choose to, rather than live in a miserable story about it.

TO ASSUME OR NOT TO ASSUME—THAT IS THE QUESTION

Once, I had to write a philosophy paper on the topic, "How Do I Know I Am Not Dreaming?" The night before it was due, I sat at my desk surrounded by crumpled pieces of paper and empty coffee mugs, cursing the absurdity of the question. "Of *course* I am not dreaming!" I wanted to shout at the professor. But I had to defend my opinion, and try to prove it. Strangely, I eventually had to admit that I did *not*, in fact, know for sure I was not dreaming. From that moment on, I was careful to remain dispassionate about my beliefs. Instead of assuming the "certainty" of something, I kept wondering, asking about, and exploring the nature of what we call "reality" (and I still do to this day).

What is an assumption made of? Wisps of stories woven from the past. In order to feel we know something, our minds weave together stories about reality. The mind is brilliant at filling in the gaps between bits of information. In fact, it is a brilliant story maker. If it does not know, it will make something up—and do it so seamlessly that we are unaware. Being aware of our minds' tendency to do this helps us ask more questions and rely less on what we *think* we know.

Can you safely assume anything? We assume things all the time—I assume the floor will be there when I get out of bed. I assume the sun will come up, too. I assume, since you are not smiling, that you are upset with me. Wait! How good is that assumption? I assume that since little Johnny got a D on his spelling test, he's not smart. Wait! How good is that assumption? I assume that all females want to be mothers and all Albanians/Russians/Americans/Christians/Hutus are _____ (fill in the blank here). Are any of these assumptions good ones, and how would we know if they are good? I assume that guy is a jerk because he cut me off in traffic. I assume something to be true because someone else told me it was. I assume the sun will rise because it always has—so it's reasonable to think it will again. But absolute certainty? Nobody can claim that.

Assuming things is efficient; we can't check everything out all the time, even if we wanted to. But when it comes to coming to conclusions about other people or cultures, or believing anything at all, we really should take a moment to check what it is we are assuming. Our assumptions about other people are made on the basis of things we learned in the past from our families, experiences, and culture. Assumptions, which come from the past, are not necessarily reflective of what is true right now. Have you ever assumed something about a person on the basis of your past experiences with that "type" of person, only to find you were mistaken? Because they spring from the past, assumptions are often a barrier to understanding others; we speak and act on the basis of the *ideas* we have *about* them instead of the people themselves, who are standing in front of us. In that way, we are not connecting with the person, but with our *idea* of them, which may have nothing at all to do with them. Thus, a connection between people is not made, and understanding, because of the barrier that assumptions create, does not occur. People making assumptions may think they understand, but they cannot, if assumptions are in place. Can we assume that rich people are greedy? We often do, but is it accurate? We can only know what our experience of a thing is in the moment we are having it. Once it becomes memory, we can't trust it entirely. Observe a day in a courtroom and how witnesses to the *same* event see different things. This is due to many factors, including our beliefs (we only see what we can believe), and how the brain receives and perceives information. If we use that same experience to predict the future, we can't trust that either—not completely. We cannot know anything for sure. It's always possible that we're wrong or that there exists a clearer picture, or a higher truth.

We once thought that objects around us were solid. When microscopes came along, we discovered that while things did act and look and feel solid to us, they really weren't solid at all—they were collections of vibrating molecules and atoms. Recently, science has told us that even that's not exactly right; everything—including humans—is a temporary collection of packets of information and energy, vibrating incredibly quickly. Science is always challenging the things we assume to be true. It's always possible that suddenly, things might change.

With respect to cultural differences between people, being aware of what we are assuming and taking for granted is very important. Since we do make assumptions all the time in order to make life a bit simpler, we need to at least know the assumptions we use should not—when it comes to concluding things about people or cultures—be relied on as accurate.

So can't we all just relax now? If none of us were sure about anything, what on earth would there be to argue about? What if we could let go of our assumptions about people and their behaviors long enough to take another look, entertain another possibility, or simply allow space for a new possibility about them to emerge? What if we could avoid assuming long enough to talk with a person and hear their point of view?

Culture Is a Story about 'Us'

The wonderful and varied cultures we live in are learned sets of ideas about ourselves and the world. They have been likened to software—mind-generated programs we pass from generation to generation.[8] They do not seem to occur "naturally." Yet we humans tend to think the way we see things is "natural" or "obvious" even though there are other cultures that do things differently. What the software comparison could imply is: it's possible for others to have different "programs," it's possible for us to *conceive* of other "programs" for ourselves, and it's possible that our own "program" is changeable.

We can understand culture as such, develop the ability to see beyond it, and thus not mistake it for who we are. Just like developing the ability to not mistake our *thoughts* for who we are, we must also learn to see that culture is derived from the mind and then become the "observer" of the culture in us.

This allows us to understand and respect culture as one of the most pervasive of belief systems, and embrace it as having specific value, while at the same time defining a new relationship to it. Culture is in many respects sacred and worthy of honor. Yet our modern reality is calling for an evolution—a shift in our self-perception as human beings that enables us to transcend belief systems or programs that limit us and our ability to connect with each other at a time in history when new solutions are needed.

---

8 Hofstede, Geert, Hofstede, Gert Jan, Mokiv, Michael, *Cultures and Organizations: Software of the Mind.* (3rd ed) (U.S.A.: McGraw Hill) 2010.

WHOSE STORY ARE YOU TAKING ON? TAKING THINGS PERSONALLY

There once lived a great warrior. Though quite old, he still was able to defeat any challenger. His reputation extended far and wide throughout the land and many students gathered to study under him. One day an infamous young warrior arrived at the village. He was determined to be the first man to defeat the great master. Along with his strength, he had an uncanny ability to spot and exploit any weakness in an opponent. He would wait for his opponent to make the first move, thus revealing a weakness, and then would strike with force and speed. No one had ever lasted with him in a match beyond the first move. Much against the advice of his concerned students, the old master gladly accepted the young warrior's challenge. As the two squared off for battle, the young warrior began to hurl insults at the old master. He threw dirt and spit in his face. He verbally assaulted him with every curse and insult known to mankind. But the old warrior merely stood there, motionless and calm. Finally, the young warrior exhausted himself. Knowing he was defeated, he left feeling ashamed. Somewhat disappointed that he did not fight the insolent youth, the students gathered around the old master and questioned him.

"How could you endure such an indignity?"

"If someone comes to give you a gift and you do not receive it," the master replied, "to whom does the gift belong?"

If you do not accept insults, but leave them where they lie—if you do not pick them up with both hands and take them into your heart—then they live with the one who delivered them. They need not belong to you, so do not attach to them.

One of the best secrets to getting along with others, avoiding conflict, and having successful interactions is not taking things personally. By this I mean not taking personally what others think; their judgements or opinions (good or bad) of you, your culture, or your family; or what they believe you should do or behave like. When you feel offended at something (when you feel bad or judged, for example), and attack or defend, you have taken it personally. You have assumed that what they are saying or doing is about you. While it may look like that, it's not true.

Everything everybody does is actually all about *them*. They are living in their own story.

If they believe a particular thing about you, why should you take their belief as your own? If they act like you are stupid, or they ignore you, what does it mean? If you are like most people, you feel bad—you feel unimportant or invisible. In response to this feeling you might become angry (how dare she treat me like I am not important!), or small (more proof I am a nobody; I'll adopt their view but secretly resent them for "making me" feel this way about myself).

If someone treats you "rudely," it does not actually mean they are rude as a person. They may be in a hurry, be distracted, or be upset by something that happened to them this morning. They may come from a direct-speaking culture, or an abrupt-style family. They act in a certain way, and your cultural conditioning interprets that behavior in a certain way (oh that's so "obviously" RUDE!), and then you add your personal stuff to it (how dare she treat me like that?). They are almost certainly not shaping their behavior specifically to make you feel bad; they are lost in their own world, thinking their own thoughts—none of which you are privy to.

But what if someone says something directly to you that is hateful or unkind? It's directed at you, right? Yes, and it's *still* not about you. If you can hang onto this you will have the greatest sense of personal freedom. Every person perceives the world in his or her own way, influenced by genetics, family, culture, and on. There are nine billion worlds on Earth. They see you through these eyes, specific to them;

the two of you could look at the same thing and see something different. What they see and think is only, only, only about them and their perspective. Being offended means we want to protect our identity—our idea of ourselves. There is no need.

—First, our idea of ourselves is, to a great extent, a cultural construct (artificial).

—Second, we are each much greater than a collection of ideas and constructs.

—Third, we need not look outside ourselves for reference points about who we are. We can allow others to think as they wish, and we may assume the same privilege. We may select the beliefs we prefer, and ignore the rest.

The value in knowing this is that you will not energize any conflict once you realize it is not about you. If you feel offended, it's due to sets of ideas you have about yourself that you have bought into, which oppose things others have bought into, and none of them is authoritatively "right." It's not about you or "your people" (being offended on behalf of others to whom you think you belong). It's just sets of ideas—why personalize an idea? You are much more than an idea.

Many people have strong opinions about lawyers, for example. I doubt I could count the number of times I've been in the presence of someone who blurted out something negative or other, like "They're all a bunch of crooks," etc. When they discover I went to law school, and was a card-carrying member of the legal profession, they often—though not always—look shame-faced and scurry away mumbling apologies. I never take offense; they either do not understand what lawyers really do and the role they fill, or they do understand and had a negative personal experience and are bitter about it. In both cases, they are attached to a story, an opinion about lawyers that has absolutely nothing to do with me, or the profession either, for that matter. It is their personal story, their experience, their baggage, which they are living in their own mind, and then projecting outward to others. I understand that the person's opinion has no bearing on the truth of the matter, and I have no obligation to buy into it. *If I became defensive, I would be granting it reality, and acknowledging its existence, even in order to disprove it.* My choice is always to express interest in their direct experience with lawyers, (often there was none) and in a light, playful way, and to offer a simple explanation about the role of the legal profession in free and democratic societies (without which we'd all enjoy far fewer liberties, but I digress...).

Consider examples in your own life where you've felt defensive about someone's opinion. You could get playful with it: in your mind, imagine them saying, "You are a polka-dotted panda!" (fill in any absurd statement you wish here, in place of their opinion). You wouldn't take that personally, would you? It's nonsensical, and you can easily see it has nothing to do with you. Why is their actual opinion any more credible than that?

Our stories, because we are meaning makers, can bring us together or force us apart. We can choose to question the stories we tell ourselves and thus open up to new perspectives. Understanding that we all tell stories, and that stories help us make sense of ourselves and the things around us, assists us in allowing others to be the way they are. If we are less attached to our own stories, we can allow others to have stories and beliefs that differ from ours. We can also be more comfortable knowing people will believe what they wish to, and while we are free to tell stories we prefer and be examples of that, we cannot control and need not try to control what others believe.

How To Accept and Allow:

b) Listen to Understand

WHAT IS LISTENING? IT'S A DANCE WITH THE OTHER PERSON IN WHICH YOU receive who they are, wrapped in gossamer layers, for you to open to the light of understanding. When we listen, we are receiving the Other. We allow them. This is because to truly listen we are setting aside judgement and mental noise—which is comprised of thoughts, opinions, assumptions, and predictions—from the past or from imaginings of the future. Listening helps us allow because it helps us understand, and when we understand, we do not judge or condemn.

We are seeing them, hearing them, and connecting with them, and by doing so, we are honoring their humanity. Listening involves interpretation and a desire to understand, which makes it distinct from hearing. There are different layers of listening. There are different purposes for listening. There are different ways to listen: with the mind, with the senses, and with the whole body. When we listen, we attend to the Other so that the sense of "I" disappears and is quiet. When we truly listen, we are open to and accepting of the Other, and we are thus allowing them.

A wise man once received a visitor from the village: a young man who talked constantly. He came seeking knowledge of all kinds. As the young man spoke, the wise man began to pour tea into a cup he had placed before his visitor. The young man noticed as he was speaking that the wise man kept pouring the tea until the cup filled, then spilled onto the saucer, and onto the floor. Still, the wise man kept pouring the tea. Finally, the young man could no longer restrain himself.

"It is too full. No more will go in!" "Like this cup," the wise man said, "you are very full of your own opinions. How can I teach you anything if you do not first empty your cup?"

We know listening is an important part of communicating. But what is communication? What is it actually for? We use it to see and be seen, to understand and be understood. Communication is essential to the human experience. People need each other, and they need communication to be together. Communication is a gift, at once bestowing the ability to know one's world, to know others in that world, and best of all, to know oneself. Much is spoken, drawn, and written, and each of these means of communicating is a study unto itself. To understand and be understood is a deep human need. Communication, whether it be through art, music, words, gestures, symbols, or body language, is all we have to achieve this.

When we cross cultures and want to build a bridge, listening is the most powerful means of connecting. When we cross cultures, we are in a place of "not knowing"; our customs, worldview, or language (which are tools we use to understand each other) is not shared. When we do not know, and we wish to build a bridge and thus become "knowers," we must listen. Listening is interpreting another's communication. As listeners, we want to *expand our capacity to understand.*

This is multifaceted, and involves attention, a quiet mind, and interpersonal skills (the ability to read context, language, nuances, nonverbal cues, etc.). It is spiritual work, really.

In the modern world, there are more and more ways to communicate. And yet, this has not resulted in better communication or less misunderstanding between people. If anything, miscommunication has increased. To be effective, a message must be received and understood by the recipient, especially in cross-cultural situations in which we often do not share the same cultural assumptions about what things mean. If I, a Canadian, am speaking with a recent immigrant from India, and I tell her to "break a leg" before she gives her presentation, she likely will not understand I mean to wish her good luck. Many casual expressions like this are meaningless or even offensive if we don't share the same cultural context.

As listeners interested in understanding and connecting with another, it is helpful if our purpose for listening is clear. Are we listening in order to receive? To understand? To interpret accurately? To know? To defuse? To connect? To learn? To respond? To listen for the sake of listening itself? To hear it all? To be open to whatever comes forward? What is your purpose? You might be listening/speaking/connecting *for* the Other (to show caring, to show understanding, to calm—in other words, to *give*). Or you might be listening *for* you (to learn, to get info, to get clear, to not get in trouble, to defuse, to grow—in other words, to *get*).

I ask my workshop participants to clarify and focus on their purpose. This lays the foundation, sets the stage, and when you are clear and allowing (not resisting), then you have a coherent energy and can harmonize easily.

ACKNOWLEDGING HUMANITY

WE CANNOT INTERPRET ANOTHER'S MESSAGE CORRECTLY—OR AT ALL—IF WE are, even unconsciously, resisting the person or what they are saying. To listen, we allow the other to be as they are, and then receive the other as they are. This is the way to wisdom and to building meaningful connections and understanding with those who are different than us.

Allowing and accepting are exemplified in the practice of compassionate listening, pioneered by Gene Knudsen Hoffman.[9] One day Gene passed by a sign in London that read, "Meeting for Worship for the Tortured and Torturers." She was astonished. As a Quaker Pacifist, she believed she should have no enemy and should care for the wounded on all sides of every battle. But it certainly never occurred

---

9   Hoffman, Gene Knudsen, Manousos, Anthony (editor), *Compassionate Listening and Other Writings* (Friends Bulletin, January 2003).

to her to put the torturers on the same level as the tortured. It was a breakthrough moment for her.

In compassionate listening, all parties are listened to deeply and their stories are understood, even if not necessarily agreed with. "A whole new chapter of my life opened. I wondered why people tortured others, and thought that if I could know that answer, there might be new possibilities for peacemaking and reconciliation," she said.

To listen compassionately is to listen without judgement and to seek the truth as it is understood and experienced by the other person. Hoffman felt that an enemy is simply a person whose story we have not heard. Compassionate listeners do not defend themselves, but accept what others say as their perceptions. By doing so, listeners validate the Others' right to those perceptions. And by listening, we validate their very being.

It is important to recognize the humanity of the other person. Not their behaviors, not their attitudes, not their ideas, not their habits—just the person. Before you, as you listen, is a human being: a complete package of contradictions, inconsistencies, hopes, dreams, fears, and strengths. People don't make sense—they never did. People are all things wonderful and nonsensical. Every person was once a baby that had no teeth, wore diapers, had a mother, cried when they fell and skinned their knee, felt frightened when alone in the dark, and learned their own special way of managing and hiding their fear. There is a small child inside every person on earth. The person before you shares almost one hundred percent of your DNA; needs food, water, and sleep; trips on stairs; and slips on ice.

I was invited to attend a church service some years ago. The minister, a woman in her midthirties, walked out into the congregation, lifted her infant son from her husband's arms, and carried him back to the podium with her. He was adorable. He was perhaps nine or ten months old, with fair curls and big dark eyes. He smiled in delight at the congregation and every heart melted. He turned to his mother and with his chubby little hands patted her face and cooed. She gently removed his hands from her face and began her sermon. As she spoke, the little boy reached up and clutched her nose; everyone gently chuckled. Again, she softly released his hand and continued her sermon. After a few minutes, he grabbed a corner of the silk neck scarf she wore and put it in his mouth. Everyone smiled. She rescued her scarf from the little one's mouth, and smiled at him. He placed his chubby arms around her neck and laid his curly head on her shoulder.

The minister said, "Take a moment to think about this: is there anything in the world you would not forgive him for?" The congregation murmured, unable to imagine looking at this child with anything other than eyes of love. You could feel them thinking of their own children and grandchildren. Then the baby shouted aloud gleefully. Everyone laughed, and so did the minister. When everyone fell silent again, she asked them, "So when does it become hard to love someone? To forgive someone? When they get older? When they are five? Fifteen? Forty? When is it that we forget that everyone is a child of God?"

It is sometimes easier to think of the love and forgiveness of a deity than to look within yourself and find it there when it's difficult. And yet, that is what empathy and understanding—and listening—asks of us.

Listening is an integration of all that is disparate within and between us. It enables acceptance and healing. By nature, it is "toward."

What does empathy mean? Many people believe that true empathy is impossible—that to "walk a mile in their shoes" involves so many assumptions and stereotypes as to make the effort pointless. My experience is that our ability to imagine a situation from another's point of view is limited, but still valuable. "If it were me..." we wonder. Even if we are mistaken, we are still trying to imagine a different point of view. This serves to soften our own position so we can really be helpful.

It helps to hold our views lightly. This true story was actually published in one of the humor sections of *Reader's Digest* many years ago: at an interdenominational religious conference in Hawaii, a Japanese delegate approached a fundamentalist Baptist minister and said, "My humble superstition is Buddhism. What is yours?"

By what standard can we judge, anyway? Every day we sort through issues: some are descriptive (how much, how many) and some are prescriptive (what you, I, or people generally "should" do). Descriptive issues are simpler, as we need only research sufficiently to find the answer. Prescriptive ones are where moral judgements live, and are a little harder. These are the ones we need to set aside when we interact with Others. Our cultures teach us what to value, and it is according to this and our personal experience that we judge. Most of us are not aware of the criteria we use to determine right, wrong, under what conditions one should behave this way or that, and for what reasons. It's a lot of work, because it involves unpacking a lot of assumptions we carry about the way the world works. Again, this is culturally derived. North Americans assume that it's "right" that everyone should have equal opportunity, but there are other ways of looking at it. Some cultures see inequality (social and economic, for example) as a natural phenomenon, and in fact, see value in it.

In addition to the complexities of judging what is proper, how can we really know what is right for someone else to do? To "know" entails knowing who they are, their experiences, their mind and heart, and "walking in their shoes." The world is full of opinions about what people should do: your mother, teachers, coaches, religious leaders, friends, and spouse each have ideas about how you should be handling things. Can they really know?

In fact, it is our minds that love to judge and assign dualistic qualities to everything: this is "good," that is "bad," etc. You may have heard the story of an old farmer who had worked his crops for many years. One day his horse ran away. Upon hearing the news, his neighbors came to visit. "Such bad luck," they said sympathetically. "May be," the farmer replied. The next morning the horse returned, bringing with it three other wild horses. "How wonderful," the neighbors exclaimed. "May be," replied the old man. The following day, his son tried to ride one of the untamed horses, was thrown, and broke his leg. The neighbors again came to offer their sympathy on his misfortune. "May be," answered the farmer. The day after, military officials came to the village to draft young men into the army. Seeing that the son's leg was broken, they passed him by. The neighbors congratulated the farmer on how well things had turned out. "May be," said the farmer.

The farmer knew that things are not always as they appear, and that, in fact, the seeds of one quality (good) are sown into the opposite quality (bad). Every event has its two opposites within it. We cannot know which is best, because "best" depends upon the context.

We cannot really know that any given event is good or bad, as the farmer's story suggests. Once we see the limitations of what we think we know, we can hold judgement (whether ours or others')—much more lightly.

Further, what can we say or judge when we have not lived another's story? It is certain that if you shared the same genes, parents, background, education, and experiences of your neighbor, you would behave the same as he or she does. We may say, "she 'should' be nicer to others," "he 'should' not cheat at poker." But by what standard shall we judge him? Yours? And why? So you can change him? Make him be different? Make him stop doing what he is doing?

Everyone does the best they can with what they know. When people know better, they do better. When we judge, we are saying we'd be different or do differently than others. If we judge others, we can start by being aware of what our judgement is, then question if it's really true, and then do whatever it is we think others should be doing. We can be the change we wish to see in the world. Rather than passively judging others' actions, you could stop wasting energy on that and instead act as an example. It starts with you, one person at a time.

LISTENING: THE GREAT DEFUSER

LISTENING VERY IMPORTANT IF WE ARE ENGAGED WITH AN "ENEMY".

I used to work in the insurance industry. After a car accident, the injured person could claim compensation for their losses, monetary and otherwise, from the insurance company. If a person insured by my company caused the accident, I'd be the agent researching and negotiating the claim. I'd often find myself across a boardroom table from them when it came time to settle the claim. By that time, I'd have a file measuring one foot thick, full of medical, vocational, and sometimes psychological reports about how the accident affected their lives. Often, this would be the first time we'd meet. The claimant almost always arrived to the meeting in a hostile or defensive mood, expecting me to be a cold, unfeeling "suit" who cared only about money. At least, that is what I imagined. At every meeting, my approach was the same: I listened. I listened with my ears, heart, eyes, and being. I tried to "feel" what they were saying and trying to convey to me. I felt that inside every one of them was a child simply wanting their pain to be seen and acknowledged. On some level, I felt they received my nonresistance like a gift. Every time, anger, fear, and aggression were gradually defused. In the face of my openness and willingness to hear them, see them, and allow them without defending or arguing, they always calmed and softened visibly. It did not always result in a settled claim, but it always calmed the roiling waters and built goodwill despite the adversarial process we found ourselves a part of.

I applied this in customer service jobs and in every situation in which opposing views had gathered steam. Just remaining nonreactive and allowing them to be who they were, and feel as they did, was enough. I often sat in silence for a time, to allow space for new information to emerge to help me make a decision about what to do. When someone is upset, they usually need to release built-up "steam," or energy, that results from the momentum of their thoughts. When I allowed space for this, and stayed silent for a time, they would often reveal in the torrent of words (which invariably came) what was really bothering them, and what they really wanted.

You can show with your body language that you understand their point of view, that you are open to them, and that you are relaxed. If appropriate, you can "soften" your body posture and the expression in your eyes. While showing interest, you can make a pause in the discussion seem expectant; lean forward as if you are waiting for something else that's coming. The power of silence is key in listening. A well-placed silence is worth twenty questions! Silence does two things: it gives the other person space to be who they are and express what is important to them, and it provides an avenue for you to gather a lot of information. Most people, certainly in Western cultures, find silence very uncomfortable, and they will do anything to "fill" it. Many times, the stream of words people use unconsciously to fill a silence reflect a great deal about their character and perspective.

LISTENING FOR THE UNSPOKEN[10]

LEO SAWICKI IS A WISE TEACHER AND MENTOR I HAVE BEEN BLESSED TO know. She traveled with the Ojibway medicine people and worked with the Cree. She also studied many traditions and philosophies pertaining to different Native American understandings of the circle of life and the medicine wheel concept of balance and healing, including those of the Shoshone tribe, the Lakota, and the Sioux. These healing traditions draw upon universal principles of Earth Medicine, and apply to all people. While aligning with no particular tribe, she works with collective teachings that apply ancient teachings to modern times.

Leo taught me much about creativity, and bringing ideas and dreams into physical form. Listening for the unspoken is part of that wisdom. On a sunny summer day, she guided me to a secluded grassy spot beside a creek in the woods in Manitoba. She told me, "Sit and *listen* to the wisdom of Nature. Let Her teach you. I will return in a while and you may share with me what you learned." I sat for hours that day; after my mind had complained about boredom and hunger and became quiet at last, I was able to open to the woodland sounds around me. The tumbling creek, whispering grasses, rustling leaves, and chattering of birds and squirrels merged gently into an exquisite symphony, surrounding me like a warm embrace. I felt like a silent part of some magical fairy-tale scene, as if I had strolled through a shimmering, translucent curtain into another dimension. I understood then that everything is intensely alive, vibrating and pulsing its very own being within some kind of beautiful dance. Because I felt like an integral whole within a larger whole, the sounds around me seemed to invite me to merge with them.

Listening can occur on many levels. We have all absently half-heard a teacher drone on through an afternoon; listened acutely for directions or our flight information in a busy airport; or listened to inter-

---

10   Leo Sawicki: http://www.leosawicki.com/

esting tidbits of information when catching up with a friend. When we selectively listen we are focused on and interested in specific things. As we move up the listening scale, we become more attuned and open to subtle energies and cues. Listening becomes subtler as it deepens. Our desire for extracting specific information is replaced by a desire for connection, which brings other subtler energies into play. There is a rich world of unspoken knowledge and feeling within and outside our standard ways of communicating with each other. Listening is a powerful portal to this other world.

The *listener becomes a midwife of sorts, allowing what is present yet unseen to come forth.* I began, that day by the creek, to learn to listen with my whole body.

When you use your body to listen, you have the ability to access universal knowledge, which extends beyond the boundaries of language or cultural customs. Not only the ears, but also the body's cells can receive information. We have access, when we deeply listen, to knowing what is intuitive, as opposed to cognitive. We can listen for what is not said, and even what *cannot* be said but is available for an immediate flash of understanding. There is vast knowledge and wisdom in between the spaces of the sounds we hear. In this, we of course are awake to context, nonverbal signals, tone, and speed of the person's speech, but there is more. We can sensitize ourselves to feel for the frequency of the person, thought, or message.

We can do this through developing our intuitive sense. Imagine driving along the road, when you suddenly know the car beside you will change lanes—you can feel it. Snipers say that their targets always know they are being watched; people have a sense, and will turn and look right at you (whereupon you avert your gaze).

Recently I wanted to change lanes on the way to pick up my daughter, but as I started, the urge came—*don't!*—so I paused, and out of nowhere a car raced up beside me on the right side, tearing off ahead in a cloud of dust. That "knowing" moment was not the product of analysis. There was no reason to pause, except a feeling I had. Driving experience helps, to be sure, and yet there was nothing in the area to trigger extra alertness.

We have a sense, and sometimes we just "know." When you are playing a sport or doing a physically demanding activity (for example, soccer), and you are totally into the game, you immediately know where to go and where to be to get the ball, to place yourself in the play. The information comes immediately; it is not a product of cognition or analysis. It is intuitive.

Everyone has this, but we rarely stop to notice. It's quiet and subtle, and it arrives in real time; then we are on to something else. If we begin to notice our "knowing" when it arrives without deliberate thought—especially knowledge that averts accidents and disaster—we'll be surprised at how often we rely on it for day-to-day snap decisions. Any time you just "know" something, your intuition is at work, helping you. It is another sense, some say the "sixth" one, reflective of the access we have to broader intelligence. It is constantly available, but if your mind is making too much noise you do not have access to this knowledge.

Intuition can be cultivated in a couple different ways:

1) First, when you have a lot of experience in a particular area, this experience forms a mental foundation—in other words, a lot of knowledge. (For example, military men and women with experience in the field have a well-developed ability to know; they can sense danger. Their knowledge provides a foundation from which they can feel if something is amiss.)

2) When you are deeply into an activity, your mind is focused on it; you have access.

3) When your mind is not making chaotic noise, you are clear—either thinking clearly, or not thinking at all.

How does intuition work in listening? Once you become present and quiet mental noise, you have access. Focus on the person: their being, their words, their signals, their underlying messages. Your intuition will let you know what is needed to "dance" with them.

The clearer your focus, the clearer your info will be. Don't think about it; know.

How does intuition work in listening to someone from a different culture? It accesses the infinite field of intelligence—where we are all connected—so there is info for you there to build a bridge. You need to get the whole picture when you are connecting with a different culture, not just isolated bits and pieces. This is because misunderstanding is a real issue; being from different cultures, you don't share the same assumptions or worldview. You need to access all available information if you are to gain valuable context and create a meaningful connection. For example, the bits and pieces of information we receive as consumers of news in the media about religious extremism and its link with terrorist activity in the world (which is currently manifesting itself most markedly in the Islamic faith community) easily leads to anti-Muslim sentiment, or at least to belief that the faith is inherently violent. This impression is deeply mistaken, but difficult to dispel without a better and fuller picture of the teachings and traditions of Islam.

Practically speaking, we cannot all delve into tomes and texts to educate ourselves properly, even if we would like to. The best we can do, as individuals, to access this whole picture is to be sincerely open to "listening for the unspoken" in our meetings and conversations with those we fear, or whose beliefs we do not understand. We do not want the bits and pieces we hear in the news to weave stories in our minds and support our mistaken assumptions that *prevent* connections that could promote understanding or healing between individuals, communities, and cultures.

When we cultivate an ability to listen for the unspoken, there is often no need for the person we are focused upon to describe themselves or their beliefs; we can *feel* who they are, and thereby connect with who they are even beyond the realm of beliefs. There is a vast amount of information we can receive intuitively, immediately, about people or situations, which bypasses our cognitive awareness completely. You might say, "I just *know*." The knowledge arrives suddenly, completely, immediately, and viscerally. There is no need for that person to drop their ideas and "meet you in the field beyond right doing and wrong doing" that Rumi referred to. It is simply required that *you* do, and that you also be willing to release the story or impression your mind has made based on the bits and pieces it has heard in the news. It just takes one person to release their attachment to their particular beliefs (which in this case often serve as barriers, as we have discussed) for there to be the possibility of meaningful connection. You can then feel who they are, where they are "coming from," and sense their being. This creates a connection between you; the other person senses they, in their innermost being, are seen, recognized, and thus validated—not for the set of ideas they have, per se, or whether those beliefs agree with yours, but for their very *existence*. As a "whole" being. Not only have you potentially built a bridge between you as individuals, and as members of different cultures, but you have expressed, by your willingness to listen for what is not said (and by accessing your deepest awareness where humanity is a shared experience), a willingness to go beyond those isolated bits and pieces of information and an openness to understanding a larger picture of their faith and their place within it. It is crucial to do this when you are reaching across a cultural divide—the bits and pieces are not enough to create understanding and connection. You need to access your sixth sense!

With proper concentration, the relinquishing of distractions, and focus, this becomes easier.

Intuition accesses the infinite field of intelligence where we are all connected; there is information for you there to build a bridge. It accesses that which is universal among us.

We can also "listen to the unspoken" by cultivating the ability to deeply listen with our bodies.

Heart listening means allowing sounds to enter your body through the heart area. Your body can listen; the heart has its own wisdom and knowledge, and this can be filtered into the interpretive process of listening. You can experiment with this by sitting quietly and listening to music by yourself, and allowing the sounds to enter through the center of your chest. Imagine the music emerging from your stereo as a series of recurring waves, extending across the entire room, which flow toward you and then past you. Now imagine that the sound waves emerging from the stereo are converging into a point, so that the waves are being funnelled directly into your chest. If you sit quietly and receive the sounds in this way, you may feel unique sensations in your chest or throughout your body (perhaps warmth, an opening-up sensation, tingling, or a lifting-up sensation). It is also possible you may feel the urge to cry. Whatever physical sensations your body does translate, you will, in any event, connect with the music more deeply and in a new way. It allows you to merge with the music and feel its essence in a way that defies words Do not worry if the exercise seems difficult at first, or if you do not feel any particular sensations in your body at first. Most of us are not accustomed to intentionally using our imaginative capacity, and it takes a bit of practice. I encourage you to cultivate this ability, however, as it brings immeasurable richness to everyday life. Be patient and kind to yourself as you practice. Once you are able to imagine the sound waves converging into your heart, pay attention to any insights or passing thoughts you receive which seem out of the ordinary for you. Often the body's "interpretation" of information is symbolic or dreamlike.

The same occurs when you engage in whole body listening—when you allow your whole body to become a resonating chamber for the music. The music, or in fact any sound, becomes not just noise and notes when you receive it through your body, but *experiences*. For example, think about what thunder is like. It is more than a sound; it is an experience. We don't just hear thunder; we *experience* it. Within that experience is perhaps darkness; the rich, expectant smell of humid air and earth; electric expectation; or deep vibration through your body, the walls, the floor...everything. The thunder is an experience that the whole body participates in—as can be anything you listen to.

When you wish to truly connect with another person, especially someone culturally different, engage your heart and/or your whole body in the communication. It requires you to be fully present and still inside yourself. You will find it easy to connect as fellow human beings because your body is able to receive the essence of the person—their being—in a way your mind cannot. You will discover a sense that you understand the essence of what they are conveying, even if you do not understand the words or symbols they use. For this experience, you can practice with music as you did earlier when you were listening with your heart. Stand in the center of the room facing the stereo. As before, imagine the music emerging from your stereo as a series of recurring waves, extending across the entire room, which flow toward you. This time, imagine that the sound waves emerging from the stereo are really tall, slow-moving waves of water, which gently contact the entire front of your body and then move right through it. Work with different imagery if that feels more comfortable for you, and be patient and kind to yourself as you practice. Again, once you are able to imagine the sound moving right through your body, pay attention to any insights or passing thoughts you receive which seem out of the ordinary for you.

We can also "listen" with our eyes. All of the information about the person—their essence—is encoded in the eyes. You can apprehend the essence of the being, and the message, beyond words. This is a subtle art, and should only be done if you truly wish to connect with the other person and you feel safe. When you open yourself to read into another's eyes, or "feel" into them, as it were, you access their soul. Look into the other person's eyes with true acceptance. There is a difference—you can feel it—between looking *at* someone's eyes (what we do in regular conversation) and looking *into* another's eyes. Keep the duration short, as this is intimate. Often this is the only route to the vulnerable, loving self within a person—to the natural love between fellow human beings. The eyes are the way past the barriers and gates we put up to shield ourselves from the world. Because eye connection is so intimate, it is usually reserved for romance. People can sense if you are trying to get "in" and will block your efforts if they do not feel safe in opening to you. If you connect in this way, trust flows more easily between you, and it creates openness, nonverbal camaraderie, and understanding that goes beyond words. At this level of connection, all people "recognize" each other; that is, they recognize the divine, or the soul, in each other. They can feel your love for them through the eye connection, and this is the strongest bridge between cultures you can build. It transcends all differences.

How to Accept and Allow:

c) Be Here and Now

"Be Here Now"

—*Ram Dass*

The Dissolution of Stories and Judgements from the Past

The present moment is the one clear, still place in which we can transcend the many barriers that exist between us, and find a bridge across the gaps to connect with each other. In the present moment, not only do we feel clear and peaceful, but that clarity and peace emanates from us and influences everyone around us, consciously or subconsciously.

But what does it really mean? It is possibly the most difficult thing to describe, because it is not a thing, and the experience of it defies words entirely. Being present for our purposes means *being* right where you are, in the experience you are having, or being completely *with* the object of your attention. Relationship Coach Selena Wright says it's "being where your feet are" (i.e. having your awareness anchored solidly within your physical body). Take a moment or two each day to notice your thoughts. You will find they jump around among things that happened in the past (a minute ago, an hour ago, ten years ago) and things you expect to happen in the future (usually worry, but also anticipation).

Have you ever awakened in the morning, calm and refreshed after a good night's sleep, and laid there in your bed a short while meaning to enjoy the moment, when suddenly thoughts of what you have to do today, or what happened yesterday, started roaming across your mind? If you are like most people, your mind seizes upon those thoughts and races off with them like a team of wild horses, dragging *you* behind! Nothing in your immediate environment has changed at all (you are still in your bed), but you have jumped from a calm and content state to feeling anxious and upset, all within seconds. The upsetting thoughts actually originate in a past situation or memory, *or* an assumption, based on past experience, which you are projecting into an imagined future (dread, for example). But the present moment simply contains you, in your bed, right where you are, inhabiting the experience of being alive in that moment. Your attention is on that—not upon things that happened in the past or what will happen tomorrow. It means not having your attention wound up in your own mental noise. In my workshops, after I enjoy a few laughs with the group about the "team of wild horses" idea (everyone can relate to it) I explain that it's important to anchor some of your awareness in your body (your feet, for example, as Selena teaches). The reason is simple: your energy follows your attention. If you move some of your attention into your body (and become aware in any given moment of the sensations on your skin, or the temperature of the air, or the softness of the chair you sit on), you actually remove attention from your repetitive thinking, and the "team of wild horses" loses power, and has less "pull." So body awareness is a powerful tool to help you remain in, or return to, the present moment. It quiets the mind, and brings us into the fullness of the moment.

When you begin working with this, your mind might shout at you, "Boring! There are other/better/more exciting things we need to be doing right now!" Most of us feel compelled to rush through time and events, conversations and minutes, to get to the "next thing." In the process, we unconsciously rush right through our lives. And yet, the present moment—right here and now where you are—is all there is.

There is nothing else, and there never was. I have sticky notes all over my office that say, "Let yourself have the gift of this moment." They remind me all day long about what is most important. When you allow yourself to fully experience the moment you are in, right here and now, no matter what shape it takes, you feel deep within what a gift each moment really is.

Interestingly, accepting and allowing others to be as they are is so much easier when we fully inhabit the present moment. Just like going away on vacation, it is like stepping away from the worrisome details of life. Problems become much clearer and much smaller. In fact, they disappear altogether, because in the present moment there is only what *is*: rather than a problem, there is simply a situation you can deal with or not, as the case may be. This nonresistant state is a natural by-product of dwelling in the present moment. In that state, conflict cannot abide.

Accepting others as they are has several advantages. First it's a relief to stop trying to correct them. It's a relief to let go of figuring out exactly what's "wrong" with them. It's a relief to not have to solve the problem. It's a relief to let go of needing to be right. It's a relief to float in what is. It's a relief to work *with* what is and with its energy, instead of against it. It's such a big job, after all, to straighten everybody out.

A simple way to access relief and be accepting is to develop your ability to be fully present. Presence is the answer to the question, "How do we lighten up, relax, and let others be?"

Being present helps us let go of the past, future, and all the unhelpful activity of our minds, like judgement. It helps us see connections that we cannot see from our regular mind. And it helps us listen, receive information more clearly, see the self in the other, and release fear, anxiety, and tension because the stress-generating mind is quiet.

Cultivation of present-moment awareness is crucial in any situation where differences between people are significant, and where there is conflict. It must precede any cross-cultural dialogue also; otherwise, we end up reenacting old programs, particularly where there is a lot of cultural history involved. The present moment, as we know, is free from past and future. It feels good to be in the present moment because no problems live there, just situations. "Situation" simply means a set of circumstances; there is no implicit judgement about them. It is neutral—could be good or bad or neither. "Problem" implies a situation that is negative, and has been around a while, and/or is anticipated to exist into the future too.

Present-moment awareness is a very simple way to transcend, even temporarily, culturally conditioned responses or any differences between people. We can transcend culture easily when we are deeply present because in that state it is possible to actually feel a connection with all things. When we are in that state there is no conflict and no "problem"; the person dwelling in the present moment is able to set down their side of a conflict (I call this "dropping the rope," referring to a tug-of-war dynamic between two sides) so there is no more tension. True connection is really born in, and lives in, the present moment.

.Observe your thoughts: they do live in the past and future, and almost never in the present moment. The past is wonderful for reflecting, making meaning of things, learning, observing patterns, taking stock, and making stories. The future is wonderful for anticipation and constructive planning. But often our thoughts of past and future are compulsive and negative, which makes them discordant, stress-inducing, and destructive to our well-being. We become unable to recognize or appreciate the present moment and the power it contains.

In the present moment, you can see, think, and receive clearly because the barriers that separate you from others temporarily dissolve. They are all based in the past; they are all ideas or thoughts that have been repeated enough that they have become beliefs. Cultural perspectives, gender, background, education—these are all aspects or layers of identity you picked up by learning from others around you.

The ego, as understood by Eckhart Tolle in *The Power of Now*, is, to me, like different cultures: an artificial construct made up of ideas born in the past, which we use to weave stories and make meaning.[11] In the present moment, when you are fully being in the here and now, you are not any of those things. You are simply being. You are clear as crystal. The messages others communicate to you flow to you directly and clearly, not refracting infinitely through all the layers through which you perceive the world. The key to the problems we face in relating across vast differences, especially cultural differences, is to go beyond the mind and its habitual patterns of thoughts—all the layers of identity and conditioning we have absorbed over time.

When we occupy the present moment fully, problems disappear and all is well, no matter how it appears. You can see a bigger view. Several times a day, I sit with an "empty" head. It clears the deck, clears the chaos in my mind, and when I pick up my activity again, I feel clear and energized. Something wonderful happens when you drop all thought and simply rest in the moment, not trying to make anything happen. The world around you steps forward and comes alive in a rich way, as if it is a part of you, and you are breathing it in. Dwelling there, you can feel as if you are one with all around you, and Life itself is living through you. It feels like everything around you is alive, and awake, and aware, and you are somehow "dancing" with it.

When you are upset, try dropping down into yourself—your body—to calm down. This removes energy from the mind, which is gathering steam, not clarity. Dig deeper down into yourself, into the present moment, before that frenetic mind energy takes root, and you

---

11   Tolle, Eckhart, *The Power of Now: A Guide to Spiritual Enlightenment.* (Novato, California: Namaste Publishing and New World Library) 1999. P. 22

will find clarity and peace. Being in the present moment gives space for emotions to simply be without you feeling you have to run off and do something about them. Have you ever gotten so angry that you suddenly lashed out at someone in fury? You were reacting automatically, without thinking (unconsciously), in response to something that, on many levels, reminded you of an event in your past. Acting "on automatic" in unthinking reaction to our habitual patterns of thought is what we do until we become present and aware. Only then can we say we are choosing our thoughts and words and actions on purpose and acting freely. Until then, we remain creatures of habit, more or less, acting in accordance with our past conditioning—what we learned from our cultures and past experiences. There is nothing wrong with that, per se. However, it is difficult to transcend barriers between people and cultures when old habits of being are still active. An elderly woman I knew was taught all her life to fear and avoid black people. Then an African family moved in next door. It took a long time for her to even leave her front porch when they were out in their yard. Over time, and with the help of their friendly entreaties and waves through the window and over the fence, her fears (which, by the way, she could not even explain the reason for) subsided. Then there came a hot summer afternoon when she looked out the window to see the neighbor woman suddenly collapse in her yard. Without thinking, she ran across to her, and soon found herself ministering cool compresses and hot tea. Years later, she told me, "You know, I brought her tea and there we sat, right there in the grass, just the two of us together. I looked in her eyes, and knew everything I thought before was wrong." In the present moment, none of the voices of the past had any power at all. The key to listening in a cross-cultural context is quieting all mental noise. Mental noise is conditioned and culture-dependent. So to connect, we simply quiet our minds.

The main reason we want to be present in the here and now is because in the present moment, there are no "old tapes" playing. There are no stories. We are not reacting automatically in response to the old tapes playing in our head about this or that person, this or that group of people. We are not listening to the tapes from our past, nor projecting those tapes into the future (in terms of what we should expect from the Other). In the present, the moment is uncontaminated by the past (history, old hurts, prior incidents) or future (anticipation, worry, dread), and instead is fresh.

So when we are present and perceiving a person or thing that is different, we are receiving that information as purely as possible, just as it is, so whatever response we have can be appropriate to that context, that person, that set of circumstances. What usually happens instead, though, is we react automatically to a person on the basis of past experience or cultural conditioning, which, as it is a product of the mind, is based in the past as well.

When we become aware that we are not *constitutionally* Albanian, female, or middle class, for example—when we loosen our identification with the various layers of "self" we are assigned by culture, etc.— we can better allow other ways of being, because we know they are all part of the tapestry and variety of life. Even things we don't like have a role in creation, and simply by their existence offer us a choice about what way we choose to focus and create something more or something different, as the case may be.

Seeing that we are larger, or more than, the layers of culture and personality we are habitually immersed in, we can more easily make *conscious* choices outside these layers of culture and personality. We can freely choose beliefs, actions, and responses for ourselves, instead of reacting according to ideas that have come from the past. With this freedom we can play with roles, cultures, and physical forms and enjoy them, without taking them too seriously. If we don't mistake them for who we really are, we don't invest in defending a way of being, and we don't find others' differences with us threatening.

The present moment does help us transcend our limited, time-bound, and identity-bound perspectives; it is a great and simple solution to bridging differences that requires only practice to master. Without present-moment practice, it is inherently difficult for anyone to step outside of his or her perspective. Being truly present expands your sense of self. When that occurs, you are more open and conciliatory. You are able to sense a connection between yourself and others that lives beyond physical appearances.

One good measure of whether you are present is whether your body is relaxed.

Are you allowing and accepting? An important part and measure of allowing—and in fact the best measure of your success—is your body. Your body is the best measure of resistance. Most people live constantly in a vague sense of unease, which is reflected in the body. We are immersed in a steady low-level stream of adrenalin generated by our anxious thoughts. We unconsciously grind our teeth, clench our jaws, and tense our muscles.

But when you are allowing, there is no tension in your body. If there is no tension in the body, there is no "holding" or resistance in the mind. Tension arises when we are thinking about something from the past or something we are expecting or projecting toward in the future; it flows from old, learned behaviors and thought patterns. We learn to "guard" against unwanted things and unwanted feelings—and unconsciously, we guard with our bodies by remaining tense. This is the same sensation as fight or flight, only it doesn't end; the body is, through the mind, immersed in a constant environment of stress. If there is tension in your body, even a small amount, you are resisting, and thus not receiving valuable information or well-being. Your body reflects what you are doing with your energy. Right now, see if you can notice any tension in your muscles, anywhere in your body. Your body always tells the truth about your mental state. If you wish to know whether you are allowing, look to your body: is it relaxed?

We need to distinguish alertness from tension in this context. Alertness is consistent with relaxation, while tension is not. The difference consists in the thought pattern involved: when you are tense, you are resistant in your thoughts. You are guarding against something. In some way you are defending against or pushing against. On the other hand, alertness feels like low-level eagerness: you are in the present moment, still, open, but there is no ongoing dialogue in your head about there being a problem to guard against. You are in a relaxed state of readiness.

Sometimes it's hard to know for sure whether we are "open," so here are some suggestions:

—Look to your shoulders: are they relaxed or tense? Tension means you are guarding against something; you are resisting, not allowing.

—Look to your breathing. Is it slow, even, and deep? Most people take small, shallow breaths—evidence of holding and tension.

Your shoulders and breathing belie your inner state.

Tension is actually a low-level manifestation of fear. Most of the time, when we feel tense, we are not actually responding to a real threat in our immediate environment. Instead, we are imagining or dreading something based on past experience, which our minds then project forward into the future. Not only is this constant state of hyper-alertness not healthy, but it also operates as a block—a physical barrier—to our natural well-being, to valuable information from our environment, to acceptance and allowing of others.

To develop the habit of allowing, it's helpful to begin by relaxing when you are alone in a low-stress environment. If you can practice it when it's easy, you'll have the skills to draw on when it's more difficult. Can you relax right now where you are?

Try this exercise. Right now, find a comfortable place to sit; choose a firm chair with a straight back. Place your hands where they are comfortable—perhaps in your lap. Take a deep breath in. Now breathe in as deeply as you possibly can, hold for ten seconds, and then release the breath fully, emptying your lungs completely. Now again: fill your lungs to their max capacity and hold...and let it go. On your exhale, allow all tension to leave your body. Allow your face, scalp, mouth, and forehead to relax. Let them drop, and let go of the tension. Relax the muscles around your eyes. Relax your arms and hands, your abdomen and pelvis. Allow all tension to flow out of your legs and feet. If it's helpful, imagine all tension from your body flowing out of the soles of your feet and into the Earth. Are you feeling a difference in your body? The tension you released represents the resistance in your mind—your resistant thoughts. Notice how much resistance you had, and how much better you feel letting it go. This is the difference between resisting and allowing. Now you have felt the difference, imagine having a conversation with someone close to you after completely letting go and relaxing. Try it and take note of the difference in your experience of the conversation, and in their response to you.

Among the many benefits bestowed by present-moment awareness is the ability to begin to see the link between thinking and feeling. Often we are so busy thinking—or allowing our minds to drag us around—that we are not really aware of how we are feeling. It's only when we are really happy or upset that we can tell. Many of us wander around all day feeling a vague sense of unease, but since we are mentally preoccupied much of the time, we either don't notice, or don't stop to question why we are feeling "off." The ability to sense how we feel is so important—not in order to find an exact label to apply to the emotions, per se, but in order to know whether we feel positive or negative, good or bad. When you look at or think about something, you need to know how that thought or observation actually feels to you, so you can move your mental energies deliberately in a direction that feels positive to you.

(So now we have made room in the world for differences, how do we work with them?)

THE PEACE OF NOT THINKING

DEEP IN THE PRESENT MOMENT, IT COULD BE SAID THAT WE ARE NOT REALLY thinking at all. We experience inner peace and a connection with all other things. We simply "are." When thoughts do arise, being in the present moment *fully* allows you to enjoy them, entertain them if you choose, or let them float by, but no thought has any emotional "pull." They are rather like background occurrences, as opposed to the driving force in life. Resistance (negativity), which is what most automatic thinking is comprised of, does not live in the present moment, so it is simpler to allow the person, the situation, the moment to be as it is. It is a peaceful state, which has a contagious effect on others around you.

Presence acts like a soft blanket of snow. Imagine standing in a silent wood one dark night in deep midwinter: silent white snow blankets the whole world as soft white flakes float down to the ground. All is deeply still: the moon, the stars, the trees. You feel like holding your breath to honor such magical silence—it feels expectant in some way. This is the feeling of being in deep present-moment awareness, and the feeling of being in the presence of someone who is. No "noise" can live there, in that kind of peace.

Once, I visited some friends for a dinner party. I was seated between two people, a man and a woman, each of whom, it turned out, felt very passionately about hunting. Or rather, one loved to hunt and the other felt hunting was abhorrent. The banter began innocently enough, but an argument took flight soon after they reached an impasse and could not agree. Lodged between them, I could actually feel a heat sensation growing as their anger mounted. Neither was prepared to acknowledge any validity to the other's points. Mediating the dispute was an option, but instead, I moved my chair back so they could speak at each other directly, and took the position of seated "bystander" with a glass of wine in my hand. They kept arguing as I rested my gaze on my wine glass, and slipped into a deep state of presence. They thought I was listening, and I was, but not to their words. Truly, they were not paying attention to me at all. Their voices were clear for a while and then became, in my mind, more like a buzz or hum. I became very peaceful inside—for me, this is accompanied by radiant joy—and within minutes, the fire went out of their dispute, and they sat quietly, not saying anything. Finally, the man said to the woman that even though he loved hunting, he was going to think about some of the interesting things she had said. She, in turn, softened and thanked him.

How To Accept and Allow:

d) Appreciation

APPRECIATION IS AN IMPORTANT PART OF ALLOWING: IT IS A GIFT YOU GIVE another. Appreciation makes allowing easier because when you look for and find qualities you admire or like in a person or thing, it's easy to feel warmer, to let down the barriers, and to stop pushing against qualities you don't like, because your attention is on what you *do* like.

1. "The Power of Appreciation"

What does *appreciation* mean? It means looking for and seeing the best in someone or something. It means paying attention to the best qualities of the person instead of the worst qualities. If you can appreciate, you are accepting and finding the good. It involves a change of thinking habit, in other words. An appreciative frame of mind can be cultivated right now: look around you and see how the light touches the objects in the room. Look out the window and see life expressing itself in myriad ways. Feel the breath flowing in and out of your lungs, sustaining your life. Notice the abundance all around you. Appreciating is easy if we just take the time to notice things—*really* notice them. Develop the habit of noticing and appreciating the simple things in your life, to provide you a strong foundation to spring from when you begin consciously appreciating people. Like the other disciplines we have discussed so far, practice strengthens your ability.

If you can appreciate others for who and what they are, you are giving them a gift. When you convey that you appreciate them, this builds trust. People come to life when they feel seen and appreciated. Simply comment, "What a unique perspective. I had not thought of that before." They will open up and share more, and be excited to convey their understanding to you. There is a little child inside everyone who wants to be seen and heard. Appreciation, like listening, extends this gift. When you appreciate, you are more open to others and to finding things in common. Appreciation is a willingness, an openness, and a moving-toward. It is a willingness to understand.

Can you sit down and appreciate everything around you and everyone around you?

Let's try it. Appreciate your body. How? Notice it, pay attention to its unique characteristics, how it functions, the jobs it does for you, the ways it helps to keep you well. Notice how it functions and takes care of all the details of keeping you alive, leaving you free to attend to other things. Notice its strengths, its abilities (walking, bending, expressing, thinking), its potential.

Appreciation is simple. We simply look at what *is* working, not at what is *not* working.

Here are some ways to bring out your ability to truly appreciate others:

—Be open to learning, to seeing differently.

—Notice others; pay attention to them, be present, and sense their being (underneath their words and actions).

—Observe them without judgement (without mental commentary).

—See them as a small child.

—Recognize them as fellow human beings and look deep in their eyes. Appreciation for their very being will fill you.

—Note the roles they play in the world. What is their job? Whatever they do, no matter what it is, is a service to their family, to their community, to humanity. Every being is important, and there are no high or low jobs—every being contributes something.

—Ask yourself, "What experiences have they lived through?"

—Ask yourself, "What do they wear, do, or say that is unique or interesting?"

—Ask yourself, "What qualities do they bring out in you?"

—Imagine how they see the world, and you.

—Consider their existence in the fabric of life.

—Try thinking that the difficulties they seem to be creating for you are really gifts.

Every person has a story, and when we take the time to look for it, appreciation of that Other comes easily. If you can look in another's eyes, you can appreciate. For when you gaze in another's eyes, you see their soul, their essence, and their soft inner core. Cultivating the ability to appreciate is the best thing you can do in the world—for yourself and for everyone you come into contact with. Can you find things to appreciate in every person?

How Do I Appreciate the 'Tough' Cases?

SOME PEOPLE ARE REALLY DIFFICULT TO GET ALONG WITH, OR TO LIKE AT ALL. The good news is we can appreciate something in everyone, even if we don't like them or want to invite them to tea. We can appreciate someone without liking them. Every coin has two sides. We need not try to make ourselves like people we can't stand. But we can extract positive things about them based on where we decide to direct our attention. And we can appreciate people even when they do not extend appreciation to us.

To appreciate people we don't like, we can:

—Look for anything about them in which we can see positive attributes. If they are loud and obnoxious, can we find it in ourselves to admire their confidence? If they are dishonest, can we contemplate their creativity? Their bravado? If they are angry, can we appreciate their passion? Their energy? If they are argumentative, why not notice their shrewdness, or persistence? A person's qualities are not necessarily good or bad—it is what we decide to find and focus on that matters.

—Remember they were once a little baby, frightened and crying.

—Remember that somewhere they have someone who loves them—a mother or father, perhaps—someone who cared for them and watched them grow.

—Expand our perspective and see they are a part of all that exists, even if we cannot understand the role they play or the value in what they contribute.

In all things and people there are opposite qualities: things you prefer and things you don't. A person you consider "good" in fact has "bad" in them as well—but they express the good much more than they express the bad. Both are present, however.

Every cloud has a silver lining, so the saying goes. Every difficulty has a gem within it. Appreciation resides in the ability to see blessings in challenges. One day I read an article that suggested that readers write down the hardest thing they ever handled in their life. I did. The next step was to name five benefits you got from that experience. They could be skills, experience, knowledge, friends, development of new qualities—anything. I thought about it. Indeed, I discovered, without the problem I had faced—and at that time was continuing to face—I'd never have learned what I did, stretched myself, started a new career, or developed self-respect. It forced me to grow in ways I certainly would have avoided if given a choice at the time. Even if we can find not one thing to appreciate in someone, we can still appreciate their role in creating a difficulty that is bringing forth the best in you.

Any difficulty is like a grain of sand within an oyster. Like the sand, which agitates against the inner flesh of the oyster, our challenges rub up against us, creating friction. This can be very painful at times. But our discomfort produces passionate desire, perhaps for freedom (get me out of here!), for relief, for escape, or simply for happiness. This desire can lead to the choices and experiences perfect for the full expression of our uniqueness. It leads to our fullest potential.

To claim that our pain or difficulties define us, however, denies the power we each have to shape our own lives and experiences.

So can we take this wisdom and appreciate the difficulties we experience—and the people who we feel are responsible for those difficulties? Indeed we can. They are our blessings; they help us grow and explore the best of ourselves. Our difficulties provide the very sharpening stones upon which we need to polish ourselves, our talents, and our gifts. Seen in this light, it is easy to appreciate others with whom we differ, especially the ones we cannot like.

Using Thought and Energy on Purpose

We have spoken about ways to allow the Other (person, culture) to be as they are, and how to allow the situation and moment we are in to be as it is. We don't worry about it, complain about it, or fight against it.

In doing this, we surrender all resistance to things or people being the way they are and believing the things they do. We fully accept, so we are free to work with the materials we actually have: the situation itself, plus the materials within our own personal control (our attention and our attitude). This is where our power lives: in the nonresistant moment—the moment in which we are thinking and feeling and experiencing. We can simply focus on things we wish to cultivate, and remove our attention from things we do not. We can become aware of our attitudes, or feelings, and so begin to harness their power and direct them toward ideas we prefer. We focus on and lean toward things we like—toward the best in others, in situations, and in differences, thereby influencing their growth. Our thoughts create our lives. Harnessing the power of our thoughts lets us harness the power of everything that flows from them: our emotions and our actions.

When we accept everything as it is, we are powerful. We are not fighting the current; we are embracing the potential within the difference and actually conserving our energy. Our energy follows our attention. By directing our thought and attitudes, we direct our energy in a more focused, efficient, and effective way. We are not expending energy complaining about or resisting something that already exists. We are using it constructively.

When we feel the power of knowing we can direct your thoughts and feelings, we do not need others to be different in order to feel better.

If you don't need others to be a certain way, you have no resistance and will not energize a conflict; you will defuse it and more easily find common ground. What if they want to take advantage? Maybe they do. Don't let that throw you off. What result do you want? Stay in line with that, regardless of whether other people have different ideas. You can recognize their divergent agenda and stay nonreactive. From that state you can make a decision to act in one way or another, *aligned* with your clear intent. You are also free to derive a positive meaning from any situation or event.

A beautiful woman I know lives in a nightmarish toxic relationship; she loves her partner but cannot withstand anymore the emotional and physical abuse he dishes out regularly. She is desperate for things to change, wonders if she has to leave, fears for her economic future if she does, and feels paralyzed with confusion and indecision. She sits alone when she can, but her mind races: "If I go here, then this will happen. If I say that, this will happen. But I can't do that because then he'll.... Of course, if I just do this, then he might do that.... If I go here I might find work, but then I'd not see my kids at all and that would be terrible because they are my life, but when I am with them he is there too, and then I have to live like that, and so maybe I better stay, but I can't..." and on and on she goes. Her mental confusion continues unabated throughout the day, and when she returns home, the face-to-face conflict with her partner is just as intense. In response to his abusive comments, and blinded by rage, she abuses back.

One day, her minister said to her, "Do not strategize. Do not analyze. It is as it is. Let him be as he is. You will not change it, or him. You know all the things you do *not* want right now. You are very clear: you do not want this conflict, you do not want to live with this person in this way, you do not want to be away from your children, you do not want to be without a job. Now, since you know what you do *not* prefer...what *do* you want? Can you direct your thought toward that?"

She thought for moment and said, "I want...well, I haven't really thought about that. I just think about all the things going wrong and that it needs to stop."

Her minister said, "And that is good, but it will keep you exactly where you are. You see, all your focus is upon things going wrong, and things that have to change, and so with *that* focus, you are only creating more of that. *What you focus on expands.* Your mind is repetitive, and will go over and over the same thought. Have you noticed how repetitive most of your thoughts are? Most people's are, but they take it as normal, so it has not occurred to most that it need not be this way, and they can do something different. It is simply a matter of *thinking deliberately instead of automatically, steering your thoughts instead of allowing them to steer you.* Try now to direct your mind to what you would like instead. What are some things you wish for your life?"

She said, "Well, I want...a loving, supportive relationship. I want a job that is rewarding and to work with great people. I want my family near me. Yes, those are the most important things." As she spoke, the tension in her face and body eased, and a slight smile came to her lips. "Yes, that's what I want, and it would be so great. So how did I get here? How did I end up in this situation? How come I am not living that? It's all I ever wanted—not like I ask for much!"

The minister replied, "The most important thing is to know what it is you really want, and start to make room for that in your thoughts, your words, and your heart. Do not worry about how you got here— that is in the past. Let the past lie where it is, and begin to turn yourself toward what you hope for."

She responded, "Well if he weren't so abusive in the way he treats me, and so unreasonable in his demands for all the stuff he wants, I'd never have to deal with this horrible situation!"

The minister said, "In the midst of conflict we think like this. You are where you are right now, and you cannot rewrite what has happened up to now. Let him be as he is. He is as he is, and you are here, now. You simply begin here, now, where you are. Now, tell me more about the things that are important to you—the things you wish for." She spoke again about the things she wanted. "Think only about these things," he suggested, "not how they will come to be, or when. Just the 'what.' Tell me about those." And she did. As she spoke, her eyes lit up, her face became lively, and she began to feel good just thinking about these hopes.

"You see," he explained, "you have just changed direction using your thoughts. You directed them in a different direction—one that you chose. And see how much better you feel. *If you practice this way of thinking, toward the things you want, especially when you are alone and not in a challenging situation, you will find your circumstances will begin to change on their own. What you focus on expands. Thought is the beginning of all things. It comes before words, and it comes before emotions, and it comes before actions. It is the root of everything in your life and in the lives of those around you. Pay attention to that and all else will align with it. Of course, when you change the nature and tone of your thought, you will be speaking different words, and acting differently as well. So very practically, your life will change, because with different thoughts, you will be different. Do not expect the world to change for you. You are the one with the power, so you should use it. We are thinking creatures, so since we do think, let us think on purpose and not by accident. Let us not permit our minds, which repeat collections of old patterns of thought, govern us."*

Formerly, she had spent her time wishing her partner would treat her differently, which only *increased* her stress because all her past attempts to control that (being sweeter, doing more to appease him, staying out of his way, etc.) had failed. But she found that by *not* wishing things were different, and instead allowing it to be as it was, and then lifting her attention from the problem to some things she *did* want to experience, she experienced two results. Conflict occurred between the two of them much less often, and when it did, it was less intense (there was less emotional power in it) and he seemed more pleasant. She also ended up getting a new job, which paid much more and helped her feel she had more options, should she choose to exercise them.

By releasing her resistance to the situation, she freed up a lot of excess energy that was going toward negative thinking.

Think about a time you were really anxious about something—a time during which you were immersed in feelings of stress for at least a day, imagining and fearing the worst would happen. You might recall how exhausting that was. You spent an enormous amount of energy: your heart rate was higher, your breathing was shallower, and your thoughts were more frenetic. The same dynamic is at work here. Often, simply freeing up this energy by releasing resistance (negativity, against-ness) is sufficient for a situation changing all by itself, because when we are more relaxed, we are less negative and reactive. The words we speak are a bit softer, and it's easier to interpret things in a more positive light.

Releasing resistance also enabled her to do even more; not only could she relax more and feel better right away, she now had the clarity to direct her mental focus in a more constructive direction. But here's the interesting thing: she did not actually *plan* to get the new job. As she tells it, it "landed on her doorstep." She could not explain exactly what it was that made her partner nicer, either.

She simply practiced accepting things as they were and directing her thoughts whenever she could toward things that *felt* better. Overall, she was feeling better and better—and it seemed the better she felt about things, the better things seemed to work out. The more she guided her thinking toward things she wanted, the better she felt in just thinking about them, and the more she found herself thinking, speaking, and acting consistently in a more positive direction. In doing so, she witnessed the conflict with her partner melting away more every day. Essentially, what she focused on—things that felt better—grew larger.

Habitually, we are used to noticing and talking about problems much more than solutions. Interestingly, when we are in the midst of stressful situations, we are often so busy looking *at* the cause of our stress—which makes our minds spin faster and faster, so we become increasingly anxious (angry, upset, etc.)—that we don't have enough clarity or calm to look away, even mentally, from the cause of stress to something more calming. We often don't have access to clear ideas about solutions, either. Like our beautiful friend, when we are in the midst of our problem, everything looks bad and it's hard to figure out a solution. So you don't need to cook up a solution right then. Instead, just allow, and direct your thoughts toward things you like, things you'd like to have happen. Imagination is a powerful and effective tool. This does a number of things: your mental clarity improves and you have better access to solutions, which will occur to you more often; you feel better in the moment, which is actually the main objective in anything you undertake (everybody is actually doing what they do, ultimately, to feel better or happier); and you are more positive toward the other person, which defuses the conflict.

PERSONAL POWER AND RESPONSIBILITY

ANY TIME YOU SAY "SHOULD," PLEASE PAY ATTENTION, BECAUSE YOU ARE resisting what is. While it might be true that your mother-in-law *should* be nicer, and people *should* be honest, and *should* not hit, yell at, or shoot others, the fact is that they do. What we think about it is irrelevant to the fact that it *is*. This is the first and most essential step.

What will you do, who will you be, in the face of this situation? Every situation is an invitation to determine what we will choose to be, and who we will chose to be, in response to it. Make your primary point of focus the quality of your response, instead of the factor you can do nothing about. You have power over your state of being.

A different response to a familiar scenario will set it spinning in a new direction. Only one ingredient needs change, and that is your response, which comes from your state of being, which in turn derives from your thoughts.

You must always work *with* what you have, not against it. Use the present moment and everything in it as raw materials with which to create something new. You will then be flowing toward solutions, not pushing against problems. While the difference may seem slight enough to be semantic, it is significant.

To claim our power and effect change, we need to use energy differently. We must become nonresistant, or allowing; we must not push against, in order to conserve and direct our energies more efficiently.

> *"Each one has to find his peace from within. And peace,*
> *to be real, must be unaffected by outside circumstances."*
> —*Mohandas (Mahatma) Gandhi (?)*

Imagine having infinite dollars and resources to build your perfect house from scratch. Anything you want. Anywhere you want. This is difficult because the deeper you proceed into the project, the more difficult decisions become—when you can do anything, what do you choose? How do you choose? The ideas are formless. There is no basis to build upon, improve, tinker with, or create more or less of. Creation asks for focus upon that which we want, and often the way we do that is to become clear upon that which we do not want. This is an integral part of the process. We need to start with something to focus upon. The direction then becomes clear. And then we can build, tear down, or modify, and....create.

What if, instead of resisting what is (our differences with others, and all other things we don't like), we welcomed it instead as an important and necessary ingredient for change and forward motion?

Welcoming differences—even using them as tools—is possible when we understand how to use our focus and attitude toward difference.

Simply put: what we focus on expands, and what we put in, we get out. What you focus on expands, and your attitude about it determines your trajectory. Choosing your object of focus and cultivating a positive orientation toward your preferred outcome is the key. In other words, thinking and feeling *on purpose* is important if you want to influence your experience in navigating differences with others. You can focus on what is wanted, not what is unwanted, and you know the difference between the two by how you are feeling. This involves conscious awareness of the emotions you are experiencing, as well as use of the power to define things in ways you prefer.

> *"To know what you prefer instead of humbly saying Amen to what the world tells you you ought to prefer, is to have kept your soul alive."*
>
> —*Robert Louis Stevenson*

Once we harness and master these principles, we have the ability to approach difference consciously and create something new intentionally. Moreover, we are utilizing our energy efficiently. Ancient martial arts traditions have long known that you must flow your energy all in one direction; to be effective in the use of our energy, we do not split it.

Diversity—of thought, emotion, action, culture, environment—is the clay in which we play. It's where experience lives. There's no joy without sadness, no knowledge of light without dark. It's how we define ourselves. Use it to define yourself, to shape your circumstances. We don't stand in the rain and whine; we get to work building a shelter—because we want to be dry and comfortable. We don't complain about there being no place to celebrate together; we create a plan and build a cathedral—because we want to have a nice place to celebrate together. But to be effective, we must not act from negativity, doing something to avoid something we don't want. We must focus on what we do want, and our action will be smooth and clear. Reach for the light (allow), don't run from the dark (push against). There's a very big difference between the two.

Unseeing the Big Dipper

One cool autumn night I was gazing into the black sky, enjoying the millions of beautiful stars on display. I wanted to simply allow the infinite display of stars to "be" in my awareness, without having thoughts *about* it, per se. I remember as a young child being able to see things without applying labels or "knowledge" about them. The whole world around me, as a child, felt filled with potential, bursting with color and vitality and possibility in every moment. The more knowledge I gathered over time, the more the aliveness of the world seemed to slip away, or become hidden from me. Even though I intended not to impose any kind of mental "order" on that night sky, my mind fastened upon the Big Dipper constellation very quickly, and I found that once I saw it, it was difficult to unsee. Once a pattern has been made in the mind, it is difficult to unmake it. So instead of taking the pattern apart, we can build new associations on to it, taking an inclusive approach. Instead of trying to get rid of a pattern in the mind, such as a belief (which is simply an established pattern of thought), we can decide, instead of fighting it, what we *do* want to believe instead. This is like the difference between problem-thinking and solution-thinking. If I am in the middle of a situation that I think is a "problem" (in other words, I am resisting the situation and being negative about it), the only options I can see will be consistent with that mindset of "problem." Seeing something as a "problem" provides scaffolding for it to replicate itself. But if I think in a solution-oriented way, I am working with what is, and looking at the situation (not judgementally) with the question, "Given this, what can I do now?" Then I am free to choose and build on something new—whichever available option I choose—and generate a completely different trajectory of thought. I am focused on *including* what I prefer, instead of *excluding* what I do not.

We can lift our focus away from something troublesome, and without trying to fight it, place our attention on something elseAnd then repeat. Instead of trying to change a pattern of thinking—which is really a belief—by trying to take it apart, grapple with it, or figure out where it came from, we can move past existing beliefs simply, by applying our attention consciously.

The Good News: It's Not Hard Work

We begin ridding ourselves of beliefs not through effort and gnashing of teeth, but by allowing and consciously directing thought—by aligning the energy we expend with the desires we hold for a better world. This is about ease and flow, not expending effort.

A young but earnest Zen student approached his teacher, and asked the Zen Master:

"If I work very hard, how long will it take for me to find Zen?" The Master thought about this, then replied, "Ten years."

The student then said, "But what if I work very, very hard and really apply myself to learn fast? How long then?"

Replied the Master, "Well, twenty years."

"But, if I really, really work at it? How long then?" asked the student.

"Thirty years," replied the Master.

"But, I do not understand," said the disappointed student. "Each time that I say I will work harder, you say it will take me longer. Why do you say that?"

The Master said, "When you have one eye on the goal, you only have one eye on the path."

The Master knows that in setting a goal, in trying to make something happen, we are adding resistance. We are making the arrival a problem, a challenge to be overcome. There is a natural ease to all endeavors when they are inspired from nonresistance and clear, directed thought.

We already expend massive amounts of energy controlling each other, controlling external events, and pushing against things we disagree with. We can become more mindful of how we use our energy, and choose ways to direct it on purpose.

CHOICE

WE MUST BE PROACTIVE AND CREATIVE WITH OUR THOUGHTS. LET'S NOT expect everything to be perfect and just as we like it. In fact, in every situation and every person, there is something we like and something we do not. Everything is this way. We have a choice: which will we focus on and align with—what we like or what we don't? The choice is ever present. We are always selecting a perspective on things, whether we are awake to that or not. Neither perspective, (positive or negative) is more right than the other, and both are present. We are each of us completely free to think in whatever direction we choose. Why not exercise our power, do something different, and choose to focus on what we prefer? The thing is: either way we will get more of whatever it is we are thinking about. Why not choose?

When we are upset, we habitually slip into automatic behaviors without even realizing it. *Every thought has a feeling attached to it.* Emotions are simply extensions of thought. If we think a thought often enough, it develops more emotional power, and we develop a standard set of responses to situations that trigger it. Someone cuts us off in traffic and a rush of emotion overtakes us; we react in the way we always have in the face of that emotional response. So when something happens that triggers an angry feeling, we launch into defensive mode, or attack mode, for example. It takes us over and we act on automatic. We are overtaken by emotion, in other words. After it has run its course, we are left to survey the damage.

But when we want to find ways to cooperate and get along with those with whom we differ, we want to have the presence of mind to choose, and then direct our energies. We want to be free to decide for ourselves, and not have automatic responses—which are based on the past and have nothing to do with the present situation—deciding for us.

We want to do all that we do on purpose. We can think on purpose, and we can feel on purpose too.

One great way to handle this is to understand that the emotion is simply a feeling, and it need not engage us completely. We can put some distance between ourselves and our emotions; we can observe them without being taken over by them. We can have the feeling and let it be there without acting on it. We see it for what it is and it passes on its own.

You are not your thoughts. They are neutral tools, really, that can be chosen, mastered, and manipulated to suit what it is you wish to live, experience, or achieve. You know you are not your thoughts because, quite simply, you can be aware of them. If you know you are having a thought, and can distinguish between thoughts, then who is thinking? It sounds absurd, but please reflect on it for a moment: you are thinking a thought. So what *is* it that is *you*? You are a being, an entity, an awareness, which can select thoughts at will. Once you really know that deeply, there is nothing you cannot do. So if you know you are not your thoughts, and you can select direct them, then you are completely free. Nothing holds you anymore.

Years ago I met an eighty-five-year-old woman—always impeccably dressed and coiffed, no matter the day, season, or weather. She was always up and dressed early every morning. She managed all this even though she was legally blind. She was in the process of moving to a nursing home, with the assistance of her children. On the big day, she waited patiently in the lobby of the nursing home. Eventually, an attendant arrived to escort her to her new room. As she maneuvered her walker to the elevator, the attendant provided a visual description of her tiny room, including the eyelet sheets that had been hung on her window. "I love it," she stated with the enthusiasm of an eight-year-old having just been presented with a new puppy.

"But you haven't seen the room yet!"

"That doesn't have anything to do with it," she replied. "Happiness is something you decide on ahead of time. Whether I like my room or not doesn't depend on how the furniture is arranged. It's how I arrange my mind. I already decided to love it. It's a decision I make every morning when I wake up. I have a choice; I can spend the day in bed recounting the difficulty I have with the parts of my body that no longer work, or get out of bed and be thankful for the ones that do. Each day is a gift, and as long as my eyes open I'll focus on the new day and all the happy memories I've stored away just for this time in my life."

You do have choice. We often say things like, "She made me angry." It feels like there are emotions and behaviors we cannot control. But it simply feels that way because you have not practiced controlling it at its root: the orientation of your thought. Nobody has control over the way you feel. And when you cultivate awareness of the relationship between your thoughts and emotions, and practice consciously choosing what you think, you will see that you do have control. You can choose what to notice about a person, and you are free to *not* notice things as well. You can lift your attention off of things that bother you. If you are *purposive* in your focus (i.e. if your purpose is to get along and find common ground), it will serve you to selectively notice things that assist in that. You can make peace one thought at a time.

Here is the power of your attention: focus on your hand. Feel it from within. Feel its aliveness. You will feel physical sensations. This is the power of your focus made physically manifest. Imagine what could happen when you consciously direct your thoughts toward peace.

The Feeling of Thoughts

My young daughter was enraged one afternoon. Her art project was "ruined" by a mistake she made with the paintbrush; she meant to paint a perfect green tree, with red flowers beneath it, but the red paint splotched onto her green tree. She became a bear in an instant. Roaring with indignation, she wanted to tear up the paper and throw it on the floor. I suggested she make it into an apple tree. She paused, nodded, and went to work, happily completing her painting with this modification in mind. I said to her later that the only difference between before (angry) and after (happy) was a thought. Notice the effects of the different kinds of thoughts on how you feel: positive thoughts and beliefs are integrative and coherent. In short, they feel good. Negative thoughts and beliefs are discordant, and segregating. They don't feel good.

Each thought is reflected in the body by a feeling. Every thought is translated physically in the body. Becoming sensitive to this is very important when you begin to guide your thoughts. Creating a bit of impartial distance from our emotions is helpful: it is just a feeling, after all, and has no power as such. The fear we feel in a given moment might *feel* real and compelling, but if there is no immediate physical threat, it's an insubstantial phantom, and once you recognize it as such, you realize you are not that, and need not be driven by that. If it is not fed by your focus, it passes on its own and need not be something we get involved in, or run away from. You can feel the feeling, allow it to be there, decide you would rather feel good, and begin selecting thoughts that feel better. Sometimes relief is the best thing to aim for. There is no need to let the negative feeling dominate—it is simply a habit of thought, and can be substituted for other ones. You are in charge. People are not accustomed to approaching emotion in this manner, but I assure you it is not necessary that we are run by our automatic responses to past events. We can consciously choose new feelings and responses.

I realize the process I am describing here sounds a bit mechanical and odd. Personally, though, I have found it exhilarating to free myself from fears that felt incredibly real. Intellectually, of course, I knew it was not "reasonable" to fear them, but as you likely know, fears do not obey reason any more than a child stops worrying once Mummy announces there's no monster under the bed.

You can choose how you feel. In every particle in the Universe there is wanted and unwanted, up and down—it is a play of opposites, in a way. So everything has both, and thus everything is, in essence, neutral. This includes all the things we love and hate. So, when confronted by a thing or a difference, you can choose to see one side or the other. You do not in ordinary consciousness see both at the same time. In the moment you feel love for something or someone, you cannot feel hate at the same time. So you can choose your perspective on a thing.

SWITCHING ON THE FLY: REPLACING NEGATIVE WITH POSITIVE

WHEN YOU ARE AWARE YOU ARE THINKING ABOUT SOMETHING THAT YOU do not wish to expand, what can you do? The best way to start is to practice thinking thoughts that feel good—those are the positive ones—when it is *easy* to do. We set the tone before the conversation even begins. Like appreciation, it is a habit that is easier with practice.

If you are not sure if a thought is positive or not, see how you feel. Your feelings tell you. What is the quality of your feeling? Being able to identify it is what I call "feeling-awareness." We cannot actually *see* our thoughts or emotions, but we know we have them, even though we cannot point to them in a physical way. Is the thought you are thinking headed in a good, constructive direction for you? You can tell by how you feel when you are thinking it.

The value of connecting thoughts to how they feel cannot be understated. So often we focus on the thought itself, and give little attention to the way it feels—the sensation it creates in the body. Every thought creates a physical response.

I realize it is not easy at the beginning to determine the "feeling-frequency" of our thoughts, but it does become easier with practice. It is a subtle art, in fact. But when you get good at it, and you have the determination to always be willing to turn your thoughts in a direction that feels good, you will find that you feel better and clearer; solutions occur to you easily when you need them; and conflict dissolves from your life. The frequency, or tone, of your thought activates automatic emotional responses that affect your responses to, and connection with, others. What you put in you will get out (positive in, positive out; anger in, anger out). Thought is creative: it shapes our words, emotions, and actions.

And when you begin using it deliberately, on purpose, toward things you prefer, and not simply in reaction to things you cannot control, you will see the power you have to influence how differences play out in your experience.

Here is an exercise: Think about a problem you have. Think about something that is going wrong in your life. Allow yourself to be "in" your problem for a few minutes. How does it feel when you think about it? Now, think about solutions to the problem. Think: what could I do to create a shift in this situation? Imagine yourself taking steps to alleviate the situation; imagine this *purely*, without the mental roadblocks you may be accustomed to associating with this issue. How does it feel when you think about that? You will find the "problem" thought feels different than the "solution" thought. The former might feel like a sick feeling in the pit of your stomach, like raw dough, while the latter might feel lighter and hopeful. Like relief.

Try to see if you can stay with the thought purely without adding any extra narration.

Pure thought: I'd like to get along with this person better.

Extra negative narration: (But...he is so unreasonable, and he has never been nice before, and it's always so discouraging to even be trying this. Why do I bother? He will never appreciate me, etc.)

Pure thought: I'd like to work with people who are positive.

Extra negative narration: (But...everyone here is just miserable, especially this guy here, and I am sick and tired of it. Why can't everybody be nicer?)

Pure thought: I want to find a solution to this situation.

Extra negative narration: (But...I have been struggling with this for so long with no hope in sight, and I have tried everything, and it's just hopeless.)

If you stay with, or focus on, the pure thought steadily for a minute, you will find you feel better. Notice your mind's habit of pulling you back into "Yes, but it won't happen" or "Yeah, but that's not *reality*." Try your best to set reality aside for the purposes of easing conflict in your life and you will see amazing results. The "reality" you are currently experiencing will change before your eyes. This is because you are doing something different in the face of the same problem. You are changing a negative trajectory to a positive one, all with a redirection of thought.

It really is simple. Just become aware of the connection between what you are thinking and what you are feeling.

Sometimes you may not be too clear on *what* you are thinking, exactly. This is normal; our thoughts often move very swiftly. So become aware of how you are feeling from time to time throughout the day, especially when you are feeling great, and especially when you are feeling bad. You can say, "I feel annoyed right now...I think. What was I thinking about?"

Even if it's still not clear, don't fret; all you have to do is choose anything at all to think about that gives you a lighter, happier feeling. Even if it's not directly about the subject you'd like to solve. When you feel more positive, your resistance lowers, your thoughts are clearer, and you find either the problems you are immersed in start to solve themselves and dissolve, or the people who are problematic move away (or you do).

If you feel good, things that match that feeling occur more often. The same occurs in reverse. Look to your own experiences in the past and you will find there is strong correlation between the things you think (which cause the way you feel) and the things that happen to you.

What is your attitude toward differences? Toward those who are different than you? This attitude determines the result you experience in your relationship with them.

It's not that we need to pretend there aren't problems, difficult people, and flaws within our personalities. There certainly are. But if we learn to focus our attention on the positive features that are emerging, then we will be encouraging that unfolding potential, instead of giving more attention to the imperfections and strengthening them.

PROBLEM-SOLVING

WE CANNOT SOLVE ANY PROBLEM ON THE LEVEL OF THAT PROBLEM. WHAT does this mean? It means that when the problem is our object of focus, we are expanding the problem, and resonating with the problem itself. It grows more arms and legs the more we look at it, delve into it, chew on it. In fact, problems and solutions actually live on different emotional "frequencies."

To have a problem, you need to be looking at something and thinking it is "going wrong." Noticing this, and having the attitude that it is not as it *should* be, is resistance. You are not allowing it to be as it is. Looking at something positive to appreciate about the situation or person, or looking at possible solutions to the situation, is a completely different state of feeling.

If you purely focus on either appreciating something or finding a solution (or both), you do not have a problem. It *is*, simply, and you are lining up—by using your feelings as guides—with the solution.

Imagine sitting with a pile of bills you have to pay, knowing you have no money with which to pay them. What does it feel like? You are likely feeling hopeless or fearful. Now imagine same scenario, but think about options that can address the problem. I could ask for a loan, I could look for a second job, I could.... Now this is where it gets a bit tricky. Usually we say, "I'd like to get another job, but it still won't pay the bills." Or "I'd ask for a loan, but I won't get it," etc. But if you focus purely on the ideas coming forward as solutions, without qualifying them and canceling them with "but," you can allow the possibility of them, and immediately you feel better. The feeling in your chest is lighter. The scenarios feel quite different!

What We Focus on Grows

What we focus on expands. Of course, the reverse is also true. If you want an argument to end, *deprive it of oxygen* (take away your focus, drop your end of the rope, surrender your need to be right and to make the other wrong). In my personal experience, I have not encountered any exceptions that I know of to the Law of Attraction: "That which is like unto itself is drawn." That which we focus on expands—in number, in power, in size, in emotional impact. Thoughts, feelings, things, people...everything. When you focus on the things that make your spouse different from you, for example, when you are annoyed, you very quickly locate more and more things to feel annoyed about, and the general feeling of annoyance grows, as does each individual item on the list of annoyances. Someone could look at his bank account and think about how there is not enough money to pay his bills, "There's not enough money, I don't have enough money, I can't pay my bills because there's not enough money." Guess what will grow. The state of not having enough money. I knew a woman who constantly talked about her disabilities arising from her car accident; during the two years I worked with her, she was rear-ended eleven more times! Observe your own life: are you able to see that what you predominantly focus on is reflected in your experience? And that the more you think about something, the bigger it grows? Notice the correlation between what you are thinking and speaking, and what you are getting.

So when we focus on things—any things, positive, neutral, or negative—they grow, and more things like that are drawn toward you. So in a setting where people are diverse, what do you want to focus on? If you think about the differences, you will perceive more and they will grow—to the point that it becomes difficult to connect. Or will you think about something else: the things you can learn from them, or things you can appreciate about them.

There are many ways to make peace with the Other. For any kind of difference (whether in regards to personality, culture, morality, etc.) there are many approaches:

—Ignore the difference, look for the best in the Other, make friends with it, and look at it in a new way.

—Focus on the present, make a new story, redefine the problem, and accept them as they are without conditions.

—Keep the discomfort "local." Keep it to your experience and the person in front of you.

—Look away.

—Look for the best.

—Accept.

A Different Story about Desire

Desire has a bad name. We are told by many that desire is the root of all unhappiness, the root of greed and selfishness. But everything in our lives occurs because of desire, whether we acknowledge it or not. We breathe because we desire life. We eat because we desire life—and taste, and pleasure, and sustenance. We have become accustomed to judging the idea of desire, but there is no reason to view it negatively. In fact, it is the fuel for all evolution and progress. We want to eat to feel better. We want more money because we think we will feel better (it will help us pay our bills, travel, get out of debt, etc.). A desire, or intention, is a way of addressing a particular need that we have— perhaps for a relationship, love, or material things. It is an impulse, a thought that we have that guides us to fulfilling that need. And our belief is that in taking care of that need, we will feel better. In fact, anything we do, we do because we want (desire) to feel better—to be happy (or happier). Here is an example:

You could say, "I want a lot of money."

"Why do you want that?" I ask.

"So I can quit my job."

"Alright, why do you want to quit your job? What will this give you?"

"So I can be with my family."

And if I ask, "Why do you want to spend more time with your family?" you could say because you will feel better (that they will be cared for, that your home will be cleaner and feel better, that you will feel good knowing they are happier having you around, etc.). So the main goal nested within all other goals is the desire to feel better, or be happy.

When you are navigating differences or conflict with someone, the same thing applies. When they are difficult to get along with, or angry, your first wish is that they be nicer or more reasonable. We have already seen, though, that we cannot insist people change the way they are, or are acting, to make us more comfortable. What we really desire in this situation is harmony—to get the result we want, to avoid conflict.

Let's revisit the idea of desire. Let us treat desire consistently with the principle of allowing: it is neutral and is not one thing more than any other. It, like anything, can be good or bad. Resisting it and denying it goes against the grain. It's not desire that's the problem; it's desire plus not having what you want and focusing on what you don't want that is the problem. Wanting and receiving is where the flow is. If you knew absolutely that whatever you wished would come true, would you try to deny your desire? Would you avoid desiring things? No. We deny (read: push against) because we don't believe we can have what we want. The truth is, we often don't have what we want because our thinking is not clear enough and we don't *believe* we can have it. Remember, we live our beliefs, and we live in the stories that are woven out of our beliefs. We are also taught it is selfish to desire things, or it's somehow wrong to desire things to happen in a certain way. Actually the problem we have with desire is twofold: attachment to a specific result, and focusing on what we don't want.

A Recipe for Success

(How to handle difficult emotions) Apply this in situations where you are in conflict with another:

a) When they are around you, try to anchor some of your attention somewhere in your body (for example, "be where your feet are"). You will recall this helps quiet your mind. Don't worry about strong feelings you might be experiencing; let the emotions be there without doing anything *about* them. Then, try lifting your attention away from the trouble, place it on something you like, and focus on that. Find something in common with the Other and focus on it. Listen. Look in their eyes. Connect with the human being, not your ideas *about* the human being. See if you can create some space between yourself and the emotions you have about the person. You can let those emotions be there still, but creating a bit of space allows for the possibility that there is a different way to feel in the situation. You can let them be right. You can remain nonreactive.

b) When they are not around you, practice feeling better. Practice seeing the situation and person in a different light (try appreciation) and cultivate that, grow that. Begin with feeling happier about any-thing in your life. Get a solid foothold into a positive frame of mind—find anything you can to feel good about. Even feeling neutral will work fine. Once established in this, you may introduce the thought of the difference/person you are dealing with. Ease into it. If it starts to feel upsetting again, back out, reestablish a positive framework, and try again. The situation is not fixed; you can influence the outcome, and you can redirect your focus and frame of mind toward the issue. It is inner work, thought work, and simply a new habit. *Visualize a happy outcome to the issue without asking how it will come about.*

The vision, which is your object of focus, will grow in power and strength, and you will find that events will organize themselves around that vision. Connect with the vision and enjoy the positive feelings you experience when you focus on it. Do not use it as a means to the end, but visualize for the sake of itself, for the sheer enjoyment of how it makes you feel. The object is to feel better without attaching to the outcome. Do not ask how, where, or who. You have developed many beliefs over your lifetime regarding what is possible and not possible. For the purposes of this exercise, let these beliefs go and see what happens.

We can control the focus, and we can control the attitude, but we cannot control the process or result in a direct *linear* fashion.

What is the point of doing this exercise when the "problem" is not around?

—To strengthen your ability to focus.

—To grow positive feelings about the person and possible outcomes. (What you focus on grows; thoughts invite things.)

—To create new mental habits; to cultivate a different set point and set of responses.

—To feel better—after all, the only reason we do anything is to feel better.

c) The most powerful approach to handling difficult emotions, however, involves *no thinking at all*. In the midst of a situation which is "pushing your buttons", remove your attention from what you perceive is the cause of the annoyance. Become fully present. Notice the physical sensation of the emotion (anger, fear, stress, anxiety, etc) within your body. Do not put any words to this. Just feel: Where is it located? Keep your attention on the physical sensation within your body. It IS localized, and you can do this. Remember, it is just a sensation you are dealing with, and it's never as bad as your mental commentary says it is. Do not think about it, do not tell any stories about it. Just feel it. What you will notice is when you put your full attention on the sensation (emotion is simply your body's response to a thought, and you can feel these directly, physically), the sensation (and thus the emotion) disappears. At this point, you can think clearly and see what the situation requires in the way of words or action, if any, on your part.

Cultivating the ability to do this will ensure you are not overtaken by your emotions, which drive your automatic reactions. You will be able to direct your thought and energy intentionally. The most important element is learning to identify the physical sensation of a bad-feeling emotion, and simply holding it in your awareness while at the same time refraining from launching into a story about it. You will not say, 'He made me so mad...' or "Nobody should treat me that way..." or "How dare they do that!...." etc. Just pay attention to the sensation of it within your body – and it resolves itself very quickly, at which point you can do what needs to be done – from a clear, non-reactive standpoint.

THE POWER OF INTENTION

There once was a confident young archery champion who loved to boast and be the best. Though he was a renowned champion, he had not tested his skills against one old Zen master who also was famous for his archery skills. The young champion hit a distant bull's-eye on his first try, thus showing his brilliant technical ability. Then he took a second shot, and split the first arrow clean through the middle. "There," he said to the old master, "see if you can match that!" Undisturbed, the master did not draw his bow, but rather motioned for the young archer to follow him up the mountain. Curious about the old fellow's intentions, the young man followed him up the mountain until they reached a deep chasm spanned by a rather flimsy and shaky log. Calmly stepping out onto the middle of the unsteady and certainly perilous bridge, the old master picked a faraway tree as a target, drew his bow, and fired a clean, direct hit. "Now it is your turn," he said, as he gracefully stepped back onto the safe ground. Staring with terror into the seemingly bottomless abyss, the young man could not force himself to step out onto the log, let alone shoot at a target.

"You have much skill with your bow," the master said, observing the young challenger. "But you have little skill with the mind that lets loose the shot."

The secret to success in navigating differences with others and creating peace is simply a bit of mental retraining: reducing inner resistance (conserving energy), and then directing thought from a point of power that is clear (directing energy). Allowing combined with purposeful, conscious intention—we must create with our thought first, not action. Thought is primary. We have thought, it comes naturally, so why not use it as a tool? Don't let it use you or drag you around like that team of wild horses. You can choose what you think about. With all the freedom in the world to do so, why would we not exercise this choice? Who says they have a better claim to your attention than what *you* determine? We think; it is natural that we do so. When we do, we want it to be in a good direction.

A martial arts student approached his teacher with a question. "I'd like to improve my knowledge of the martial arts. In addition to learning from you, I'd like to study with another teacher in order to learn another style. What do you think of this idea?" "The hunter who chases two rabbits," answered the master, "catches neither one."

What You Put in You Get Out

What you reap, so you shall sow. One day, a farmer brought his eldest son out to the fields. He held out two seeds resting in the palm of his hand. "Son, this land will all belong to you someday. The soil in these fields is rich and deep. This soil does not mind one way or the other what you plant in it; you can plant beans, peas, hot peppers, or trees. It always offers you choice, and is not concerned about what you choose. Like Nature herself, it is indifferent. It will return what you plant, but doesn't care what you plant." He held out two seeds: "This one is corn, and this one is nightshade. Which will you choose to plant? One is healthy to eat, the other is deadly. The soil will nurture each equally, and does not mind."

This soil is like your mind, and like the whole Universe itself. It will return you, again and again, to yourself. If you plant a corn seed, nurture it with water, and let it bask in the sun, you will in time have a plant that will nourish your body. If you plant a nightshade seed, nurture it with water, and let it bask in the sun, you will in time have a plant that, if ingested, will poison you and everybody you feed it to. If you have positive thoughts, and you give them attention (water and sun), they will grow and provide you with positive feelings, and positive results. You will think, feel, decide, and act on the basis of the "thought-seeds" that you water in your mind. A miserable journey does not yield a happy ending.

But if you smile, the world smiles back at you.

If I stood in front of a mirror with an angry expression on my face, and I wanted to see a different expression on my face, would I try to reach into the mirror to rearrange the expression? No. I would look to myself—the point of origin—for the expression to change. Don't expect the reflection to change. Plant different seeds.

ONE PERSON AT A TIME

THE LITTLE WILL BE GREAT

CHANGE BEGINS ONE PERSON AT A TIME, ONE THOUGHT AT A TIME, ONE CHOICE at a time.

We often feel helpless and discouraged as we see conflict over differences in the world, and even experience it within our own lives. It feels like there is nothing we can do to bring about peace, and we feel, "what, as one little person, can I do?" We might feel like creating peace on earth is too monumental a task to hope for in this lifetime—or any lifetime. A philanthropist I know stated with certainty, "It will take at least five hundred years for things to change." This may become true if we allow ourselves to believe it—but it need not be so. We can allow for miracles, and for the power of the individual to alter the course of events. We can individually be the change we wish to see in the world." President Barack Obama said, "Peace must be made between people, not just governments."

A recent radio program hosted four international experts in cultural conflict and immigration in the wake of a terrorist attack. These were some of the best minds in the field: highly intelligent, extensively published, well-respected. It was a pleasure to listen to their collective brilliance and analysis of the problems and hostilities besetting many nations around the world. They all wanted change and improvement, increased acceptance and tolerance among people, and an end to the violence. It became clear to me as I listened to the program that their intellectual brilliance was more of an impediment, however, than a help. They were so expert at fine distinctions and subtle concepts that even finding agreement on the *definition* of the problem (or what should be done, what should be addressed, what is working, the nature and effects of the problem) evaded them. The complexity of even *defining* the interwoven issues was impossible, let alone agreeing upon the solutions!

Our minds tend to create problems when we do not use them deliberately; the barriers between individuals and between cultures are mind-made, not "real," per se. Differences and conflict between people exist because of the thoughts, ideas, labels, and meanings we assign to them. We become lost in the problem, and less able to orient ourselves in the direction of solutions. Solutions will not come from the "Ivory Tower," policymakers, or institutions created out of mental concepts, but from the hearts and minds of individual people, one by one.

Now is the time for ordinary individuals, rather than governments, leaders, and the intellectual elite, to determine the course of human history. The power of one individual to influence the course of world events, simply by thinking and acting in a new way, is beyond measure. It just takes one person willing to allow another, or to transcend the influence of culture, to choose a new thought and a new way in order to begin positive change.

Humanity is now awakening to its true power and potential. When this is apprehended within each person, a new world opens before us.

JUST ONE HEART

JUST ONE HEART CAN CHANGE EVERYTHING. WE HAVE ALL SEEN A HARDENED face melt in the light of a loving smile, a scowl dissolved by the kindness of a listening ear.

There was once a man who used to go to the ocean to do his writing. One day he was walking along the shore, preparing his mind for a day of writing. Far ahead of him on the beach, he saw a human figure moving like a dancer. As he got closer, he saw that it was a young girl who was not actually dancing, but reaching down, over and over, picking up starfish on the beach and throwing them back into the ocean. The man said, "Why are you throwing starfish in the ocean?"

The girl replied, "The sun is up and the tide is going out. If I don't throw them back, they'll die."

"But there are miles and miles of beach here, and thousands of starfish all along the way. You can't possibly make a difference!"

The girl listened politely, bent down, picked up another starfish, and threw it into the water, past the breaking waves, and said, "It made a difference to that one!"

Once, there was a boy who was devoted to his God. He was filled with passion about learning from the great masters and putting into practice all he learned. But the more he learned, the more he compared himself: when he learned of the great, inspiring tales and deeds of these masters, he felt he could never be that great, or be as great a light to the world as they. But then his mentor said to him, "Do not behold them with your physical eyes only. Look at them through the eyes of your soul. When you do, you will see the light in them is the same as the light in you and in all the masters you admire. Maybe your light is small, but it is the same as the light in all. Keep reaching until your light fills the whole world."

A conscious change on the part of one person is powerful, and reverberates across the whole universe. Like ripples extending out from a pebble thrown in a pond, a new choice, a new thought, a new action touches one person, which changes how he or she interacts with another, and affects every choice flowing throughout the course of the day, and that person's life, and all those that person touches. A choice to smile at a person in line at the grocery store could alter the course of their day—or life. A young teen secretly planning suicide suddenly, in that moment, finds she is seen, and that she matters, and that there is hope in this world. We all have a choice to love instead of throwing a stone—to reach out a hand instead of blaming.

Let us begin it now.

CPSIA information can be obtained at www.ICGtesting.com
Printed in the USA
LVOW07s0332131015

457976LV00015B/180/P